FREE Study Skills DVD Offer

Dear Customer,

Thank you for your purchase from Mometrix! We consider it an honor and privilege that you have purchased our product and want to ensure your satisfaction.

As a way of showing our appreciation and to help us better serve you, we have developed a Study Skills DVD that we would like to give you for <u>FREE</u>. **This DVD covers our "best practices" for studying for your exam, from using our study materials to preparing for the day of the test.**

All that we ask is that you email us your feedback that would describe your experience so far with our product. Good, bad or indifferent, we want to know what you think!

To get your **FREE Study Skills DVD**, email <u>freedvd@mometrix.com</u> with "FREE STUDY SKILLS DVD" in the subject line and the following information in the body of the email:

    a. The name of the product you purchased.

    b. Your product rating on a scale of 1-5, with 5 being the highest rating.

    c. Your feedback. It can be long, short, or anything in-between, just your impressions and experience so far with our product. Good feedback might include how our study material met your needs and will highlight features of the product that you found helpful.

    d. Your full name and shipping address where you would like us to send your free DVD.

If you have any questions or concerns, please don't hesitate to contact me directly.

Thanks again!

Sincerely,

Jay Willis
Vice President
<u>jay.willis@mometrix.com</u>
1-800-673-8175

CDL Exam

CDL Practice Tests & Air Brakes Endorsement

SECRETS

Study Guide
Your Key to Exam Success

CDL Test Review for the
Commercial Driver's License Exam

Published by
Mometrix Test Preparation
CDL Exam Secrets Test Prep Team

Written and edited by the CDL Exam Secrets Test Prep Staff

Printed in the United States of America

Mometrix offers volume discount pricing to institutions. For more information or a price quote, please contact our sales department at sales@mometrix.com or 888-248-1219.

Mometrix Test Preparation is not affiliated with or endorsed by any official testing organization. All organizational and test names are trademarks of their respective owners.

ISBN 13: 978-1-5167-0794-2

Dear Future Exam Success Story:

Congratulations on your purchase of our study guide. Our goal in writing our study guide was to cover the content on the test, as well as provide insight into typical test taking mistakes and how to overcome them.

Standardized tests are a key component of being successful, which only increases the importance of doing well in the high-pressure high-stakes environment of test day. How well you do on this test will have a significant impact on your future, and we have the research and practical advice to help you execute on test day.

The product you're reading now is designed to exploit weaknesses in the test itself, and help you avoid the most common errors test takers frequently make.

How to use this study guide

We don't want to waste your time. Our study guide is fast-paced and fluff-free. We suggest going through it a number of times, as repetition is an important part of learning new information and concepts.

First, read through the study guide completely to get a feel for the content and organization. Read the general success strategies first, and then proceed to the content sections. Each tip has been carefully selected for its effectiveness.

Second, read through the study guide again, and take notes in the margins and highlight those sections where you may have a particular weakness.

Finally, bring the manual with you on test day and study it before the exam begins.

Your success is our success

We would be delighted to hear about your success. Send us an email and tell us your story. Thanks for your business and we wish you continued success.

Sincerely,

Mometrix Test Preparation Team

TABLE OF CONTENTS

Top 20 Test Taking Tips

1. Carefully follow all the test registration procedures
2. Know the test directions, duration, topics, question types, how many questions
3. Setup a flexible study schedule at least 3-4 weeks before test day
4. Study during the time of day you are most alert, relaxed, and stress free
5. Maximize your learning style; visual learner use visual study aids, auditory learner use auditory study aids
6. Focus on your weakest knowledge base
7. Find a study partner to review with and help clarify questions
8. Practice, practice, practice
9. Get a good night's sleep; don't try to cram the night before the test
10. Eat a well balanced meal
11. Know the exact physical location of the testing site; drive the route to the site prior to test day
12. Bring a set of ear plugs; the testing center could be noisy
13. Wear comfortable, loose fitting, layered clothing to the testing center; prepare for it to be either cold or hot during the test
14. Bring at least 2 current forms of ID to the testing center
15. Arrive to the test early; be prepared to wait and be patient
16. Eliminate the obviously wrong answer choices, then guess the first remaining choice
17. Pace yourself; don't rush, but keep working and move on if you get stuck
18. Maintain a positive attitude even if the test is going poorly
19. Keep your first answer unless you are positive it is wrong
20. Check your work, don't make a careless mistake

General Information

Most states will use a multiple choice CDL test format. This means you will be given a question followed by several possible answers. Usually there will be three to four choices. You are to choose one answer and mark the appropriate selection. This is for the written test only. There will also be a practical (driving) test that will accompany your written test scores. Some states will have laws specific to their state regarding CDL acquisition. Check with your state to find out any state specific laws that they may have. You can usually find this information on your state's DMV or DPS website. This manual does NOT provide information on all the federal and state requirements needed before you can drive a commercial motor vehicle (CMV). Information on CMV operation requirements may be obtained from your state's department of transportation, or the Federal Motor Carrier Safety Administration (FMCSA).

Getting your CDL

When you apply for your CDL, you must show proof of your identity, social security number and residency. You must also provide your most recent medical examiner's certificate. You are required to hold a CDL instruction permit a minimum of 30 days or show successful completion of a DMV or Department of Education approved CDL driver education course. If you already have a driver's license, you can use it as proof of your identity, social security number (dependent on state), and residency. If you do not have a driver's license, you generally must provide the following:
- 2 proof of identity documents, such as a driver's license, birth certificate, government issued photo identification card, CDL instruction permit, unexpired U.S. military identification card or U.S. military discharge papers. You must provide original or duplicate documents. Photocopies will not be accepted.
- 1 proof of your social security number, such as your social security card, IRS W-2 form, payroll check or check stub, unexpired U.S. Military identification card. Photocopies will not be accepted. If you do not want your social security number to be displayed on your license, DMV will issue a control number for your use.
- 1 proof of residency, such as a payroll check or check stub, voter registration card, IRS W-2 form, U.S. or state income tax return. Residency documents must show your name and the address of your principal residence in as it appears on your application for license.

If you are required to meet FMCSA regulations, you must provide your most recent medical examiner's certificate. Medical forms are available at any DMV or DPS office. All drivers must certify that they are in compliance with the Federal Motor Carrier Safety Administration regulations, or that they do not have to comply with them. Refer to the FMCSA regulations for an explanation of these safety requirements.

Vision standards

To operate commercial motor vehicles, you must have:
- 20/40 or better vision in each eye, and
- 140 degrees or better horizontal vision.

These visual requirements must be met without the aid of a telescopic lens. Some drivers may be granted waivers from these vision requirements. For information concerning waivers for travel

intra-state, contact your local DMV or DPS. For information concerning waivers for travel inter-state, contact the Federal Motor Carrier Safety Administration at:
Federal Vision & Diabetes Exemptions, MC-PSP Division 400 Seventh Street SW, Room 8301 Washington, DC 20590-0001.

Commercial motor vehicle

A commercial motor vehicle is:
- a single vehicle with a gross vehicle weight rating (GVWR) of 26,001 pounds or more
- a combination of vehicles with a gross combination weight rating of 26,001 pounds or more if the vehicle(s) being towed has a GVWR of more than 10,000 pounds
- vehicles that carry 16 or more passengers, including the driver
- any size vehicle that transports hazardous materials and that requires federal placarding.

Commercial drivers

Commercial drivers refer to anyone that operates commercial motor vehicles in a paid or volunteer position. Mechanics who test drive commercial vehicles must also meet commercial driver's license requirements. Commercial driver's license requirements do not apply to the following:
- emergency vehicle operators, such as EMS or firefighters
- active duty military personnel operating military vehicles
- operators of farm vehicles when
    - operated by farmers
    - used to move farm goods, supplies or machinery to or from their farm
    - not used as a common or contract motor carrier, and
    - used within 150 miles of the farm
- vehicles operated by persons only for personal use, such as recreational vehicles and moving van rentals.

CDL age requirements

You must be at least 18 years of age to hold a CDL. Under federal law, you must be a commercial driver at least 21 years of age to drive across state lines, transport hazardous materials or transport interstate freight within the state. Your license will have an indication that you are restricted to intrastate driving.

CDL instruction permit

The first step in obtaining your CDL is obtaining a commercial driver's license instruction permit. It is similar to a learner's permit you may have had as a teenager. To obtain a CDL instruction permit, you must first pass a CDL general knowledge exam and any other exams for the vehicles that you plan to operate (e.g. Tanker, Passenger, HAZMAT, Triples, Doubles, etc.). Some of these endorsements may also combine to make one endorsement. Once you have been issued your permit, you are only able to use it when accompanied by a fully licensed driver with the same endorsements for which you are training. Often times when you are attending a driving school, there will be multiple permit holders and one fully licensed driver/instructor.

CDL classifications

The classification of what type of CDL you will need is dependent upon the vehicle you plan to operate. To determine which class pertains to you, review the following descriptions. In the following descriptions, GVWR refers to Gross Vehicle Weight Rating, and GCWR refers to Gross Combined Weight Rating.

Class A
Any combination of vehicles with a GCWR of 26,001 pounds or more if the vehicle(s) being towed have a GVWR of more than 10,000 pounds. Vehicles in this class include:
- tractor-trailer
- truck and trailer combinations
- tractor-trailer buses

If you hold a class A CDL and you have all required endorsements, you are also permitted to operate those vehicles listed in classes B and C of this section.

Class B
Any single vehicle with a GVWR of 26,001 pounds or more. Any single vehicle with a GVWR of 26,001 pounds or more towing another vehicle with a GVWR of 10,000 pounds or less. This class includes:
- straight trucks
- large buses
- segmented buses
- trucks towing vehicles with a GVWR of 10,000 pounds or less

If you hold a class B CDL and you have all required endorsements, you are also permitted to operate those vehicles listed in class C of this section.

Class C
Any vehicle that is not included in classes A or B that carries hazardous materials or is designed to carry 16 or more passengers, including the driver.

CDL endorsements

- H: Hazardous Material
- N: Tank Vehicle
- P: Passenger
- S: School bus
- T: Double/Triple Trailer
- X: Combination of N and H (as mentioned in the section on permits)

CDL restrictions

The letter code for restrictions will vary by state and not all states have the same amount of restriction codes. You can find out what your state's CDL restrictions are by contacting your DMV or DPS office via their website, telephone or in-person visit. Please note that in-person visits may take longer due to potential waiting times at your nearest location.

Moving violations

If you receive two or more moving violations within the average 5-year life of your CDL license (driving either a private or commercial vehicle) you must retake all written exams applicable to your CDL license.

Taking the CDL tests

All persons seeking a CDL are required to take a written test as well as a practical (driving) test. All CDL classifications will require a general knowledge exam. You will also need to take a test for transporting cargo. If you are going to operate a vehicle with air brakes, you will need to also take a test specific to their operation. If you choose not to take the air brakes test, there will be a restriction code placed on your CDL indicating that you cannot operate any vehicle with air brakes. If the vehicle you plan to operate is a combination vehicle, you will need to complete the corresponding test. To determine which of these sections you need to focus on for your CDL, refer to the table below.

Class A, B, C	General Knowledge/Transporting Cargo
Air Brake Vehicles	Air Brakes
Class A Combination	Combination Vehicles
T	Doubles and Triples
N	Tanker Vehicles
H	Hazardous Material
P	Passenger
S	School Bus
X	Tanker Vehicles/Hazardous Material

There will be a fee to take your exams. The frequency of how often you can test for your written exams will vary by state. Some states may also have a retest fee. You can find out any testing fees and retest information by contacting your state DMV or DPS office.

The general knowledge exam will determine how familiar you are with operation commercial vehicles. You will see things similar to your first driving exam (e.g. street signs, lights, etc.). You will also encounter specific CDL questions. Using the information you learn from this guide and any experiences from a training program, try to select the best answer. Once you pass the required written exam(s), you can take the skills exams that test your practical knowledge of what you have studied. These exams include three areas:
- pre-trip inspection (be thorough)
- air brakes (if applicable)
- on-road driving (control, shifting, turns)

You must take the skills exams in the type of vehicle for which you want to be licensed. Skills exams are not necessary for all additional endorsements, but are for some. You will need to check with your DPS office prior to testing whether or not your endorsement will require a skills test.

Tip: When backing for your test, (GOAL) Get Out And Look before you back.

Disqualifications

If you are convicted of any of the following violations while operating a commercial motor vehicle, you will be disqualified or prohibited from driving commercial motor vehicles in the future. You will lose your CDL for at least one year for a first offense for:
- Driving a CMV if your breath or blood alcohol concentration is 0.04 or higher.
- Driving your personal vehicle or CMV under the influence of alcohol or a controlled substance.
- Refusing to undergo breath or blood alcohol testing whether in CMV or in personal vehicle.
- Leaving the scene of an accident
- Committing a felony involving the use of a motor vehicle.
- Driving a CMV when the CDL is suspended, revoked, cancelled, or disqualified.
- receive a second conviction for one of the violations listed above; or,
- Causing a fatality through negligent operation of a CMV.
- Driving a CMV in possession of a controlled substance.

You will lose your CDL for at least three years if the offense occurs while you are operating a CMV that is placarded for hazardous materials. You will lose your CDL for life for a second offense, or if you use a CMV to commit a felony involving controlled substances. You will be out-of-service for 24 hours or more if any trace amount of BAC is found less than 0.04. As you may have noticed, the limitations for CDL holders are much stricter than those that operate normal cars and trucks.

Serious violations

Serious traffic violations are speeding 15 mph or more above the posted limit, reckless driving, erratic lane changes, following a vehicle too closely, traffic offenses involving fatal or injury producing traffic accidents, driving without a CDL or having a CDL in the driver's possession, and driving a CMV without the proper classification of CDL or endorsements. There are many more violations for those transporting hazardous materials. These will be explained in the hazardous material section. If you operate a vehicle on some state's roadways, you agree to take a chemical test upon request to determine if you are driving under the influence of alcohol or drugs. This is called implied consent.

General Knowledge

Inspection of vehicle

Safety is a vital reason to perform inspections on your vehicle. Inspecting your vehicle thoroughly for any mechanical problems can prevent breakdowns or accidents. Pre-trip inspections are required by both federal and state laws. Federal and state inspectors can inspect your vehicle at anytime without your permission. The consent is implied when you obtain your CDL. If they find your vehicle to be unsafe, they can put you out of service until the problems have been repaired. If you are convicted of violating an out-of-service order, your CDL may be suspended or revoked. There are three kinds of inspections:
- pre-trip (before operating the vehicle)
- during the trip (watching gauges, mirrors and at each stop)
- post-trip (when you have completed your driving for the day)

Things to watch for during your trip:
- Tires, wheels and rims (check chains in snow travel)
- Brakes (can become overheated in mountain descent)
- Lights and reflectors (make sure all lights are functioning properly)
- Brake and electrical connections to the trailer
- Trailer coupling devices (check the seal on the couplings)
- Cargo covers and tiedowns (make sure hooks are secure during travel)

It's a good idea to inspect your vehicle within the first 25 miles of the trip and also every 150 miles or every 3 hours.

> *Tip: If your couplings aren't sealing well, moisten the connections. Also make sure there is always enough grease on your 5th wheel to ensure a solid trailer connection.*

Inspect your vehicle at the end of your day. If you find any problems with your rig, report them to your dispatcher. They will usually try to find local assistance for you as soon as possible. Make note of things that could be potential issues in the future that you may need to discuss with a mechanic at your company's local yard or truck stop.

What to look for
- Check for proper tire pressure using an air pressure gauge or by hitting them with a mallet. (you are feeling for bounce back from the mallet strike) Look for:
    - Mismatched tire sizes
    - Cuts or other damage to the tires
    - Dual tires touching
- Damaged rims or wheels
- Damage, looseness or rust to lug nuts
- Missing clamps or spacers
- Bent or cracked lock rings

Brakes: Look for brake drum and shoe problems on front, rear and trailer brakes:
- Cracked drums
- Shoes or pads with oil, grease or brake fluid on them
- Shoes worn thin, missing or broken

Steering system

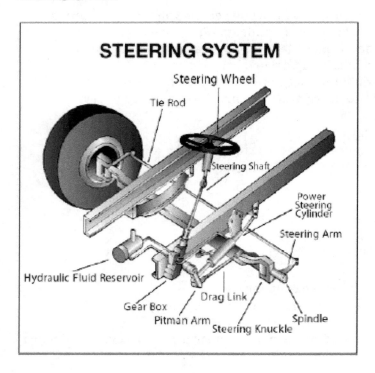

Look for:
- Missing nuts, bolts, cotter keys or other parts on the steering box
- Bent, loose, or broken parts, such as steering column, steering gear box, or tie rods.
- If power steering equipped, check hoses, pumps, and fluid level; check for leaks.
- Steering wheel play of more than 10 degrees (approximately 2 inches movement at the rim of a 20-inch steering wheel) can make it hard to steer.

Suspension system

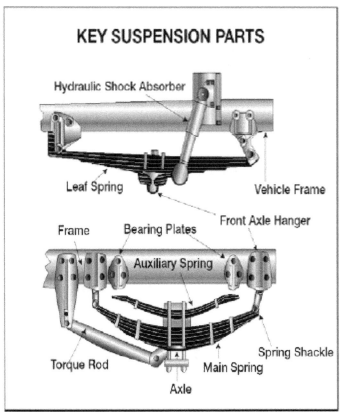

KEY SUSPENSION PARTS

Hydraulic Shock Absorber

Leaf Spring

Vehicle Frame

Front Axle Hanger

Frame

Bearing Plates

Auxiliary Spring

Torque Rod

Main Spring

Spring Shackle

Axle

SAFETY DEFECT: BROKEN LEAF IN SPRING

Broken Leaf

Main Spring

Axle

The suspension system holds up the vehicle and its load. It keeps the axles in place. Therefore, broken suspension parts are very dangerous. Look for front, rear and trailer suspension defects:

- Spring hangers that allow movement of an axle from the proper position
- Cracked or broken spring hangers
- Missing or broken leaves in any leaf spring. If one fourth or more are missing, your vehicle could be put "out of service". But, any defect is dangerous.
- Broken leaves in the multi-leaf spring or leaves that may have shifted to where they are hitting tires or other parts
- Leaking shock absorbers
- Torque rod or arm, u-bolts, spring hangers or other axle positioning parts that are cracked, damaged, or missing
- Air suspension systems that are damaged and or leaking
- Any loose, cracked, broken or missing frame members

Exhaust system defects: Damage to the exhaust system can potentially let poison fumes into the cab or sleeper berth.

- Loose, broken, or missing exhaust pipes, mufflers, tailpipes, or vertical stacks.
- Exhaust system parts rubbing against fuel system parts, tires, or other moving parts of vehicle.
- Loose, broken, or missing mounting brackets, clamps, bolts, or nuts.
- Any leaking parts of the exhaust system.

Emergency equipment

All commercial vehicles must be equipped with emergency equipment including:

- Fire extinguisher(s).
- Spare electrical fuses (unless equipped with circuit breakers).
- Three reflective triangles

Highly recommended equipment for all drivers:

- Tire chains
- Tire changing equipment
- List of emergency phone numbers
- Accident reporting kit (usually provided by employer).

Cargo

Make sure your truck is not overloaded for its rating/permits. Be sure that the cargo is balanced and secured before each trip. Also, if you are using load locks, make sure they are in place before transport. If the cargo contains hazardous materials, make sure you have all proper documents and placards for the load.

Steps for vehicle inspection

Before inspecting your vehicle, make sure that you have set parking brakes and that the wheels are chocked. If you have to tilt the cab (cabover trucks), secure loose items in the cab so they will not fall.

Step 1

Review the last vehicle inspection report. Drivers may have to make a vehicle inspection report each day. The motor carrier must repair any items that affect safety. The motor carrier must certify on the report that the repairs were made or that they were unnecessary.

Step 2

Check the engine compartment:

- Engine oil level
- Coolant level in radiator, condition of hoses
- Power steering fluid level; hose condition (if equipped)
- Windshield washer fluid level
- Battery fluid level, connections and tie downs (battery may be in different location)
- Automatic transmission fluid level (engine must be running)
- Check belts for tightness and wear (alternator, water pump, air compressor)
- Learn how much "give" each belt should have when adjusted right, and then properly check each one.
- Leaks in the engine compartment--fuel, coolant, oil, power steering fluid, hydraulic fluid, battery fluid
- Cracked, worn electrical wiring insulation.

When you have completed this part of your inspection, be sure to lower and secure hood, cab, or engine compartment door. It is very important to make sure the latches are all secure before operation the vehicle.

<u>Step 3</u>
Start the engine and inspect the inside of the cab:
- Get in and start engine
  - Make sure parking brake is set on both truck and trailer (red and yellow knobs), if applicable.
  - Put gearshift in neutral, or park if your transmission provides that option.
  - Start engine and listen for anything abnormal (grinding, whining, etc.).
  - If equipped, check the Anti-lock Braking System (ABS) indicator lights. The light on the dash should turn on and then off. If it stays on, the ABS is malfunctioning and should be reported immediately. For trailers, if the yellow light on the left rear of the trailer stays on, the ABS is not working properly and should also be reported immediately.

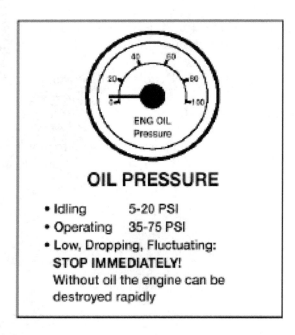

OIL PRESSURE
- Idling   5-20 PSI
- Operating   35-75 PSI
- Low, Dropping, Fluctuating:
  STOP IMMEDIATELY!
  Without oil the engine can be
  destroyed rapidly

- Check all gauges:
  - Oil pressure will take time to rise but should come up to normal within seconds after the engine is started. Some older models may take longer.
  - Ammeter and/or voltmeter should be in normal range.
  - Coolant temperature. Should begin gradual rise until normal level.
  - Engine oil temperature. Should begin gradual rise until normal level.
  - Warning lights and buzzers should go out right away.
  - Air pressure should build from 50 to 90 psi within a 3 minute time frame. Increasing the RPM will cause air pressure to rise to normal levels (around 120-140 psi)
- Check all controls for looseness, sticking, damage or improper setting.
  - Steering
  - Clutch
  - Accelerator (gas pedal)
  - Brake controls:
  - Foot brake
  - Trailer brake (if applicable)
  - Parking brake
  - Retarder controls (if applicable)

- o Transmission controls
- o Interaxle differential lock (if applicable)
- o Horns (air and normal)
- o Windshield wiper blades and washer function.
- o Lights:
- o Headlights
- o Dimmer switch
- o Turn signals
- o 4-way flashers
- o Clearance, identification, marker light switches
- o Parking lights
- Check all mirrors and windshield. Look for cracks, dirt, illegal stickers or other potential obstructions to your view. Make any necessary adjustments.
- Check all emergency equipment
  - o Fully functional fire extinguisher
  - o Spare fuses on hand
  - o Three reflective triangles and/or road flares
  - o Make sure that your safety belt is not frayed or torn and that all latches work properly.
- You will also want to inspect any optional equipment
  - o Tire chains (for snowy/icy conditions).
  - o Equipment for changing tires if needed.
  - o Tire chains (for snowy/icy conditions)

When you have completed all checks inside the cab, turn your engine off and test all of your lights outside of your vehicle. Make sure that your parking brakes are set and your key is removed from the ignition.

Step 4
Make a walk-around inspection:
- Check that all lights are working as mentioned above.
- Check the front left side
  - o Driver's door glass
  - o Door latches
  - o Left front wheel
  - o Left front suspension
  - o Left front brake
  - o Left fuel tanks (check tank straps for wear)
- Front
  - o Front axle
  - o Steering system
  - o Windshield
  - o Lights and reflectors
- Front right
  - o Front right checks (same areas as front left)
  - o Right fuel tanks (check tank straps for wear)
  - o Condition of all parts inspected
- Transmission
  - o Exhaust system

- o Frame and cross members
- o Air lines and electrical wiring—look for snagging, rubbing, wearing
- o Spare tire carrier or rack
- o Spare tire and/or wheel securely mounted in rack
- o Spare tire and wheel (proper size, properly inflated)
- Cargo securement
  - o Cargo properly blocked, braced, tied, chained.
  - o Tailboards up and properly secured.
  - o End gates free of damage, properly secured in stake sockets.
  - o Canvas or tarp (if required) properly secured to prevent tearing, billowing or blocking of either the rearview mirrors or rear lights.
  - o If vehicle is oversized, check that all required signs (flags, lamps and reflectors are safely and properly mounted and that you have all required permits
  - o Make sure all compartment doors are securely closed, latched or locked and that required security seals are in place.
- Right rear
  - o Wheels and rims
  - o Tires
  - o Suspension
  - o Brakes
  - o Lights and reflectors
- Rear
  - o Lights and reflectors
  - o License plate
  - o Splash guards
  - o Cargo securement
- Left side--Check all items checked for the right side. Also check:
  - o Battery(s) if they are not mounted in the engine compartment
- Check all signal lights.

Step 5
Start the engine and check the brake system:
- Hydraulic brakes
  - o If the vehicle has hydraulic brakes, pump the brake pedal 3 times.
  - o Apply firm pressure to the pedal and hold for 5 seconds.
  - o The pedal should not move.
  - o If it does, there may be a leak or other problem. This must be fixed immediately.
- Air brakes
  - o If the vehicle has air brakes, build air pressure to 100-120 psi. Turn off the engine, release all brakes.
  - o Press hard on the foot brake and hold down for one minute.
  - o On combination vehicles, air pressure should not drop over 4 psi.
  - o On single vehicles, air pressure should not drop over 3 psi.
  - o Turn ignition on.
  - o With the foot brake, pump the air pressure down. At about 60 psi, the low air buzzer should sound.
  - o Keep pumping air down with foot brake. At about 40 psi, the tractor parking brake knob and the trailer parking brake knob should pop out.

- Parking brakes
  - Set the parking brake.
  - Put the vehicle in low gear and gently release the clutch until you feel the tractor pulling against the brake.
  - The vehicle should not move.
- If operating a bus, additional things to check are:
  - the passenger entry
  - seating
  - emergency exits
  - baggage compartment
- If you are driving a tractor trailer, also check:
  - catwalk
  - all parts of the coupling system (5th wheel lower plate, etc.) You will not be able to see the lower plate if the vehicle is hooked up.
  - trailer-front side and rear (air/electrical connections, header board, landing gear, etc.)
  - Make sure the crank handle to your landing gear is secure to avoid any potential hazards from it hanging. Also make sure your gear is lifted all the way.

If you find anything wrong during any step of your inspection, make sure it is fixed before operating your vehicle. It is against federal law to operate an unsafe vehicle. Make sure to wear your safety belt at all times and always watch your mirrors.

During your test, you will be required to point out the areas of the vehicle as instructed and you may even be asked what problems that area could have during an inspection. What is tested varies by state. Key things to focus on for passing your test:
1. Air brake test
2. Pre-trip inspection
3. Use of mirrors
4. Shifting
5. Turning

There are many others that are also of vital importance. These are some of the most important to make sure you know before testing.

Basic Control of Your Vehicle

Skills

To operate any vehicle safely, you must know how to control its speed and direction. This is especially true of CDL drivers because of the size of their vehicles. The following is a list of skills that you will need to understand extremely well before operating your vehicle:

- Accelerating
- Steering
- Shifting gears
- Backing
- Braking
- Constantly checking your mirrors

Ultimately, these skills need to be mastered, not just understood. They will ensure safe driving for you and the motorists around you. Always remember to fasten your seatbelt before operating any vehicle.

Accelerating

Partly engage the clutch before taking your foot off the brake (unless fully automatic). Too little or too much and you will stall. Use the parking brake when on an incline to keep from rolling back. Release it only when you have enough power to keep from rolling back. If you are operating a tractor-trailer with a trailer brake hand valve, you can use it to keep from rolling back. The trailer brakes can be a much safer method if equipped. You want to slowly accelerate to prevent jerking of the vehicle. If not done properly, your truck will stall. If you are pulling a trailer, the jerking can damage the coupling. Make sure to pull slowly and try to feel when the trailer has engaged. These steps are especially important in conditions where traction may be poor, such as in rain, sleet, or snow. If you do not follow these steps in these conditions, the drive wheels will spin, causing you to lose control of the vehicle. If you feel your wheels start to spin, slowly let off of the accelerator until you find traction. With the use of tire chains, chances of your drive tires spinning are decreased.

Steering

Hold the steering wheel with both hands. Your hands should be on opposite sides of the steering wheel. Avoid sharp motions to the steering wheel; this could cause your vehicle to whip due to its length.

Shifting gears

Correct shifting of gears is very important. If you can't get your vehicle into the right gear while driving, you will have less control and may have a more difficult time stopping.

Shifting up
Double clutching is the most common method used by those learning to shift. It is commonly used in truck driving schools.   This is the basic method:

- Take your foot off the accelerator. Push in the clutch and shift into neutral.

- 16 -

- Release the clutch
- Let the engine slow down the RPMs required for the next gear (usually 1000 RPMs slower but this can vary from truck to truck.).
- Push in the clutch and shift to the higher gear.
- Let off the clutch and push the accelerator as you would on takeoff.

This method of shifting will take a lot of repetition and practice. You can't stay in neutral too long or you will not be able to engage the next gear. If this happens, speed up your RPMs to engage the next gear. Do not force it. If you can't execute the shift, go back to your original gear and try again.

Shifting down
- Release accelerator, push in clutch, and shift to neutral at the same time.
- Release clutch.
- Press accelerator, increase engine and gear speed to the rpm required in the lower gear.
- Push in clutch and shift to lower gear at the same time.
- Release clutch and press accelerator at the same time.

Pedal operation is very similar for shifting up or down. You just need to know when you need to shift and what the RPMs should be for each shift.

Tip: Shifting down can help when you are having trouble stopping.

Special conditions where you should downshift are:
- Before starting down a hill. Slow down and shift down to a speed that you can control without using the brakes hard. Otherwise the brakes can overheat and lose their braking power.
- Before entering a curve. Slow down to a safe speed, and downshift before you enter the curve. This allows you to use some power through the curve to help the vehicle be more stable while turning. It also allows you to speed up as soon as you are out of the curve.

Backing safely

When operating your vehicle, you are not able to see everything behind you, which makes backing very dangerous. Try to avoid backing whenever possible. When you must back, do so properly. Follow these simple steps:
- Map the path you will follow when backing. Get out and look (GOAL) is very important when backing, during your road test and in everyday driving.
- Turn on four-way flashers and sound your horn before backing to ensure that all bystanders are clear, and to let other vehicles know that you are backing.
- Do not back fast. There is no room for error if you do. Use the lowest reverse gear.
- You always want to driver's side back whenever possible. This means backing with full view of the driver's side of the vehicle. The other way is considered "blind side backing" and can lead to more accidents. Whenever you have no other way, try to find a spotter to aid you when backing.
- Even in driver's side backing, if you have someone that can spot you in backing, utilize them. They can check all of your blind spots for you and signal directions to you. Your spotter should always stand where he or she has a view of the rear of the truck and where the driver can see them. If you lose sight of them during your backing, stop until you know their location. They may be in an area where they could be injured. Before you begin backing,

agree on hand signals that you both understand. Audible directions are not always possible given the loud noises of the trucks and loading docks.

Backing with a trailer

When backing vehicles without trailers, you turn the steering wheel in the direction that you want the back of your vehicle to go. When backing with a trailer, you need to turn the steering wheel in the opposite direction. To follow the trailer during your backing, you need to turn in the direction the trailer is going. This will straighten the position of your truck with the trailer. Whenever possible, always try to back in a straight line. If you have no other option and must back on a curved path, always back to the driver's side so you can see the path of your trailer. Remember to back slowly. Always use your mirrors. They help you see if the trailer is staying on the proper path or not. They also make it easier to see when corrections need to be made. Whenever you need to make a correction that cannot be done with small turns of the steering wheel during backing, pull up and realign your truck and trailer with your target. Pull up as often as you need to ensure that you back in properly.

Retarders

Retarders help slow diesel vehicles, reducing the need for using your brakes. They reduce brake wear and give you another way to slow down. There are four types of retarders:
- Exhaust
- Engine
- Hydraulic
- Electric

All retarders can be turned on or off by the driver. The power can also be adjusted on some vehicles. When activated, retarders reduce the engine power once you take your foot off the accelerator completely. If you are pushing the accelerator, it will not reduce power. Do not use your retarders in inclement weather where slippery conditions are present, especially if the unit is empty or lightly loaded. Because these devices can be noisy, some city ordinances do not allow use of them within city limits. You should see signs saying "No Engine Breaks" or something similar.

Mirrors

Use all of your mirrors to check the traffic around you and your vehicle for any problems (flat tires, fire, cargo straps, etc.). Using your mirrors is especially vital when turning, changing lanes, or merging. Do not lose focus on the road ahead. Use your mirrors to check your tires. If you are carrying open cargo, use the mirrors to check that all of your straps or chains are still secure. Also, look for a flapping or ballooning tarp. All of these things are very important to check often. Many vehicles have curved mirrors that show a wider area than flat mirrors to help with blind spots. Everything in a curved mirror appears smaller and farther away than it really is. Make sure you adjust all of your mirrors before each trip as they may have been moved at some point. They are your lifelines.

Planning ahead

Stopping or changing lanes may take a lot of distance. You must know what the traffic is doing at all times from all sides of your vehicle. Experienced drivers plan ahead by looking far in front of them so they can estimate how much room they have to make any necessary moves in traffic. On the highway, most drivers look approximately ¼ of a mile ahead. When you plan ahead, look for traffic, road conditions, sharp pavement drop-offs and signs. Also look for slow-moving vehicles. Be especially careful when driving through work zones or when you see a law enforcement vehicle on the shoulder. Do not focus solely on what is in the distance. You want to scan constantly all around you and in the distance. Once you are accustomed to doing this, it becomes routine.

Communication

Signaling

It is important to let others know what you are doing on the road. You should always use your vehicle to communicate with other drivers. Just as you would with a car, you will use your headlights, turning signals, etc. Signaling what you intend to do is important for safety. Here are some general rules for signaling:

- Signal ahead
    - Signal early
    - Signal before you turn, merge or change lanes.
    - Brake early and slow gradually for turns.
    - Flash your brake lights to warn other drivers that you need to slow down or stop. Don't stop suddenly.
    - Turn off your signal after you make the turn, merge or lane change (not all vehicles' signals turn off automatically after the turn).
    - Use your emergency flashers when moving slowly (less than 45 mph on most freeways) or when you are parked.
    - Do not signal other drivers to pass you. They cannot see around you and it could lead to an accident.
- Always pass with caution
    - Check your side mirrors for surrounding traffic.
    - Determine if you have sufficient room to pass.
    - Use your turn signal early so that vehicles from behind know of your intentions.
    - Always check the surrounding traffic again before beginning your pass.
- Communicate your presence to others
    - Whenever you are about to pass a vehicle, pedestrian, or bicyclist, assume they don't see you.
    - Drive carefully enough to avoid a crash even if they don't see or hear you.
    - At dawn, dusk, in rain, or snow, you need to make yourself easier to see.
    - Turn on your lights. Use the headlights, not just the identification or clearance lights.
    - Use the low beams; high beams can bother people in the daytime as well as at night.
    - Use your horn only when needed. Otherwise, your horn may scare others.

- When you stop on the side of the road:
  - Turn on your 4-way emergency flashers.
  - Place reflective triangles or flares within 10 minutes of stopping.
  - See the following images:

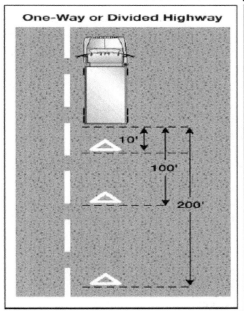

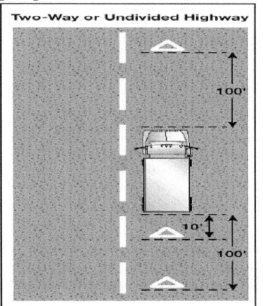

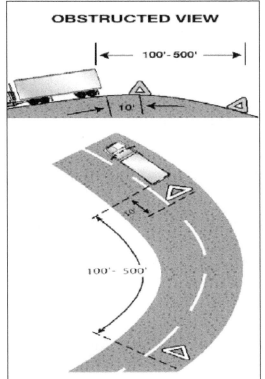

When putting out the triangles, hold them between yourself and the oncoming traffic for your own safety (So other drivers can see you). It could save your life.

Space Management

To be a safe driver, you need space all around your vehicle. When things go wrong, space gives you time to think and to take action. To have space available when something goes wrong, you need to manage space. While this is true for all drivers, it is very important for large vehicles. They take up more space and they require more space for stopping and turning.

Space ahead

You need space ahead in case you must suddenly stop. According to accident reports, the vehicle that trucks and buses most often run into is the one in front of them. The most frequent cause is following too closely. Remember, if the vehicle ahead of you is smaller than yours, it can probably stop faster than you can. You may crash if you are following too closely. One good rule says you need at least one second for each 10 feet of vehicle length at speeds below 40 mph. At greater speeds, you must add 1 second for safety. For example, if you are driving a 40-foot vehicle, you should leave 4 seconds between you and the vehicle ahead. In a 60-foot rig, you'll need 6 seconds. Over 40 mph, you'd need 5 seconds for a 40-foot vehicle and 7 seconds for a 60-foot vehicle. To know how much space you have, wait until the vehicle ahead passes a shadow on the road, a pavement marking, or some other clear landmark. Then count off the seconds like this: "one thousand- and-one, one thousand-and-two" and so on, until you reach the same spot.

Examples:
- If you are driving a 40-foot vehicle at speeds under 40 mph, leave 4 seconds between you and the vehicle ahead. One second for each 10 feet of vehicle length = 1X4 or 4 seconds.
- If you are driving a 40-foot vehicle at speeds over 40 mph, leave 5 seconds between you and the vehicle ahead. One second for each 10 feet of vehicle length plus an additional second for safety: 1X4 = 4 plus an extra second for safety = 5 seconds.
- If you are driving a 60-foot vehicle at speeds under 40 mph, leave 6 seconds between you and the vehicle ahead. One second for each 10 feet of the vehicle length = 1X6 or 6 seconds.
- If you are driving a 60-foot vehicle at speeds over 40 mph, leave 7 seconds between you and the vehicle ahead. One second for each 10 feet of vehicle length plus an additional second for safety: 1X6 = 6 plus an extra second for safety = 7 seconds.

Remember that in inclement weather, these times increase greatly.

Space behind

You can't stop others from following you too closely. But there are things you can do to make it safer:
- Stay to the right. Heavy vehicles are often tailgated when they can't keep up with the speed of traffic. This often happens when you're going uphill. If a heavy load is slowing you down, stay in the right lane if you can. Going uphill, you should not pass another slow vehicle unless you can get around quickly and safely.
- Dealing with tailgaters safely. In a large vehicle, it's often hard to see whether a vehicle is close behind you.
- You may be tailgated:

- When you are traveling slowly. Drivers trapped behind slow vehicles often follow closely.
- In bad weather. Many car drivers follow large vehicles closely during bad weather, especially when it is hard to see the road ahead.
- If you find yourself being tailgated, here are some things you can do to reduce the chances of a crash.
- Avoid quick changes. If you have to slow down or turn, signal early, and reduce speed very gradually.
- Increase your following distance. Opening up room in front of you will help you to avoid having to make sudden speed or direction changes. It also makes it easier for the tailgater to get around you.
- Don't speed up. It's safer to be tailgated at a low speed than a high speed.
- Avoid tricks. Don't turn on your taillights or flash your brake lights. Follow the suggestions above.

Space to the sides

Commercial vehicles are often wide and take up most of a lane. Safe drivers will manage what little space they have. You can do this by keeping your vehicle centered in your lane, and avoid driving alongside others. You need to keep your vehicle centered in the lane to keep safe clearance on either side. If your vehicle is wide, you have little room to spare. There are two dangers in traveling alongside other vehicles:
- Another driver may change lanes suddenly and turn into you.
- You may be trapped when you need to change lanes.

Find an open spot where you aren't near other traffic. When traffic is heavy, it may be hard to find an open spot. If you must travel near other vehicles, try to keep as much space as possible between you and them. Also, drop back or pull forward so that you are sure the other driver can see you.

Strong winds
Strong winds make it difficult to stay in your lane. The problem is usually worse for lighter vehicles. This problem can be especially bad coming out of tunnels. Don't drive alongside others if you can avoid it.

Space overhead

Hitting overhead objects is a danger. Make sure you always have overhead clearance.
- Don't assume that the heights posted at bridges and overpasses are correct. Re-paving or packed snow may have reduced the clearances since the heights were posted.
- The weight of a cargo van changes its height. An empty van is higher than a loaded one. That you got under a bridge when you were loaded does not mean that you can do it when you are empty.
- If you doubt you have safe space to pass under an object, go slowly. If you aren't sure you can make it, take another route. Warnings are often posted on low bridges or underpasses, but sometimes they are not.
- Some roads can cause a vehicle to tilt. There can be a problem clearing objects along the edge of the road, such as signs, trees, or bridge supports. Where this is a problem, drive a little closer to the center of the road.

- Before you back into an area, get out and check for overhanging objects such as trees, branches, or electric wires. It's easy to miss seeing them while you are backing. (Also check for other hazards at the same time.)

Space below

Many drivers forget about the space under their vehicles. That space can be very small when a vehicle is heavily loaded. This is often a problem on dirt roads and in unpaved yards. Don't take a chance on getting hung up. Drainage channels across roads can cause the ends of some vehicles to drag. Cross such depressions carefully. Railroad tracks can also cause problems, particularly when pulling trailers with a low underneath clearance. Don't take a chance on getting hung up halfway across.

Space for turns

Because of wide turning and offtracking, large vehicles can hit other vehicles or objects during turns. When turning right:
- Turn slowly to give yourself and others time to avoid problems.
- If you cannot make the right turn without swinging into another lane, turn wide as you complete the turn. Refer to the diagram. Keep the rear of your vehicle close to the curb. This will stop other drivers from passing you on the right.
- Don't turn to the left as you start the turn. The driver behind you may think you are turning left and try to pass you on the right.
- If you must cross into an oncoming lane to make a turn, watch out for vehicles coming toward you. Give them room to pass or stop. However, don't back up for them. You could hit the vehicle behind you.

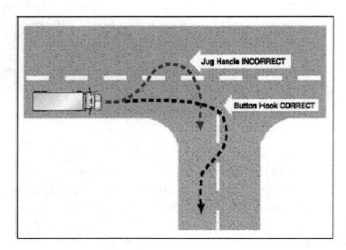

When turning left:
- Reach the center of the intersection before you begin your turn. If you turn too soon, your vehicle could hit another vehicle because of offtracking.
- If there are two lanes, always use the right turn lane. Don't begin a left turn in the left lane because you may have to swing right to complete the turn. You can see drivers on your left easier than those on your right.

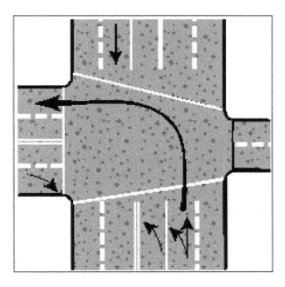

Space to cross or enter traffic

Be aware of the size and weight of your vehicle when you cross or enter traffic.
- Because of slow acceleration and the space large vehicles require, you may need a much larger gap to enter traffic than you would in a car.
- Acceleration varies with your load. Allow more room if your vehicle is fully loaded.
- Before you begin across a road, make sure you can get all the way across before traffic reaches you.

Controlling speed

Driving too fast is a major cause of crashes and fatalities. You must adjust your speed to suit weather conditions, the road (such as hills and curves), visibility and traffic.

Speed and stopping

Three things add up to total stopping distance:
>   Perception distance
>   Reaction distance
>   Braking distance
> = Total stopping distance

- Perception distance is the distance your vehicle travels from the time your eyes see a hazard until your brain recognizes it. Keep in mind certain mental and physical conditions can affect your perception distance. It can be affected greatly depending on visibility and the hazard itself. The average perception time for an alert driver is 1¾ seconds. At 55 mph this accounts for 142 feet traveled.
- Reaction distance is the distance you will continue to travel, in ideal conditions; before you physically hit the brakes, in response to a hazard seen ahead. An average driver has a reaction time of ¾ second to 1 second. At 55 mph this accounts for 61 feet traveled.
- Braking distance is the distance your vehicle will travel, in ideal conditions; while you are braking. At 55 mph on dry pavement with good brakes, it can take about 216 feet.
- Total stopping distance is the total minimum distance your vehicle has traveled, in ideal conditions; with everything considered, including perception distance, reaction distance and braking distance, until you can bring your vehicle to a complete stop. At 55 mph, your vehicle will travel a minimum of 419 feet.

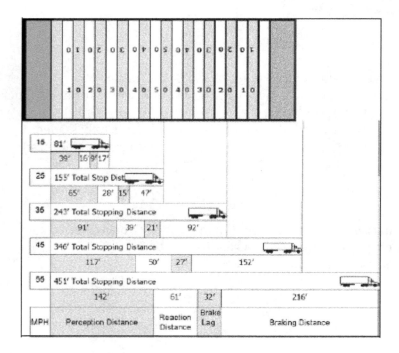

Things to remember:
- When you double your speed, it takes four times as much distance to stop your vehicle.
- Your vehicle will have four times the destructive power in a crash.
- You can't steer or brake a vehicle unless you have traction. Traction is the friction between the tires and the road. Reduce your speed on wet and slippery roads.
- Wet roads can double stopping distance. Reduce your speed by about 1/3 on a wet road. For example slow down from 55 mph to 35 mph.

- On packed snow, reduce your speed by ½ or more.
- If the road is icy, reduce your speed to a crawl. Stop driving as soon as you can.
- Empty trucks require greater stopping distance. An empty vehicle has less traction. The brakes are designed to control the maximum weight of the unit; therefore, the brakes lock up more readily when the trailer is empty or lightly loaded. This can cause skidding and loss of control.

Slippery surfaces

- Shady parts of the road will remain icy and slippery long after open areas have melted.
- When the temperature drops, bridges will freeze before the road will. Be especially careful when the temperature is close to 32 degrees Fahrenheit.
- Slight melting will make ice wet. Wet ice is much more slippery than ice that is not wet.
- Black ice is a thin layer that is clear enough that you can see the road underneath it. It makes the road look wet. Any time the temperature is below freezing and the road looks wet, watch out for black ice.
- An easy way to check for ice is to open the window and feel the front of the mirror, mirror support, or antenna. If there's ice on these, the road surface is probably starting to ice up.
- Right after it starts to rain, the water mixes with oil left on the road by vehicles. This makes the road very slippery. If the rain continues, it will wash the oil away.

Hydroplaning

In some weather, water or slush collects on the road. When this happens, your vehicle can hydroplane. It's like water skiing--the tires lose their contact with the road and have little or no traction. You may not be able to steer or brake. You can regain control by releasing the accelerator and pushing in the clutch. This will slow your vehicle and let the wheels turn freely. If the vehicle is hydroplaning, do not use the brakes to slow down. If the drive wheels start to skid, push in the clutch to let them turn freely. It does not take a lot of water to cause hydroplaning. Hydroplaning can occur at speeds as low as 30 mph if there is a lot of water. Hydroplaning is more likely if tire pressure is low, or the tread is worn. (The grooves in a tire carry away the water; if they aren't deep, they don't work well.) Road surfaces where water can collect can create conditions that cause a vehicle to hydroplane. Watch for clear reflections, tire splashes, and raindrops on the road. These are indications of standing water.

Speed and curves

Drivers must adjust their speed for curves in the road. If you take a curve too fast, two things can happen. The tires can lose their traction and continue straight ahead, so you skid off the road. Or, the tires may keep their traction and the vehicle rolls over. Tests have shown that trucks with a high center of gravity can roll over at the posted speed limit for a curve. It is always best to slow to a safe speed when taking large curves. Don't ever exceed the posted speed limit for the curve. Remember, the posted safe speeds are meant for cars. Slow to a safe speed before you enter a curve. Braking in a curve is dangerous because it is easier to lock the wheels and cause a skid. Be in a gear that will let you accelerate slightly in the curve. This will help you keep control. When you must use low beams, make sure to slow down.

Speed and distance ahead

You should always be able to stop within the distance you can see ahead. Fog, rain, or other conditions may require that you slow down to be able to stop in the distance you can see. At night, you can't see as far with low beams as you can with high beams.

Speed in traffic

When you're driving in heavy traffic, the safest speed is the speed of other vehicles. Vehicles going the same direction at the same speed are not likely to run into one another. In many states, speed limits are lower for trucks and buses than for cars. It can vary as much as 15 mph. Use extra caution when you change lanes or pass on these roadways. Drive at the speed of the traffic, if you can without going at an illegal or unsafe speed. Keep a safe following distance. The main reason drivers exceed speed limits is to save time. But, anyone trying to drive faster than the speed of traffic will not be able to save much time. The risks involved are not worth it. If you go faster than the speed of other traffic, you'll have to keep passing other vehicles. This increases the chance of a crash, and it is more tiring. Fatigue increases the chance of a crash. Going with the flow of traffic is safer and easier.

Speed on downgrades

Your vehicle's speed will increase on downgrades because of gravity. Your most important objective is to select and maintain a speed that is not too fast for the:
- Total weight of the vehicle and cargo.
- Length of the grade.
- Steepness of the grade.
- Road conditions.
- Weather.

If a speed limit is posted, or there is a sign indicating "Maximum Safe Speed," never exceed the speed shown. Also, look for and heed warning signs indicating the length and steepness of the grade. You must use the braking effect of the engine as the principal way of controlling your speed on downgrades. The braking effect of the engine is greatest when it is near the governed rpms and the transmission is in the lower gears. Save your brakes so you will be able to slow or stop as required by road and traffic conditions. Shift your transmission to a low gear before starting down the grade and use the proper braking techniques. Please read carefully the section on going down long, steep downgrades safely in "Mountain Driving."

Work zones

Speeding traffic is the number one cause of injury and death in roadway work zones. Observe the posted speed limits at all times when approaching and driving through a work zone. Watch your speedometer, and don't allow your speed to creep up as you drive through long sections of road construction. Decrease your speed for adverse weather or road conditions. Decrease your speed even further when a worker is close to the roadway. Not only is this saving the lives of the workers, but remember that tickets for speeding in work zones are nearly double that of a normal ticket. It pays to slow down.

Braking

If someone suddenly pulls out in front of you, your natural response is to hit the brakes. This is a good response if there's enough distance to stop, and you use the brakes correctly.

Controlled braking
With this method, you apply the brakes as hard as you can without locking the wheels. Keep steering wheel movements very small while doing this. If you need to make a larger steering adjustment or if the wheels lock, release the brakes. Re-apply the brakes as soon as you can. You never want to lose control while braking. It is important not to panic.

Stab braking
- Apply your brakes all the way.
- Release brakes when wheels lock up.
- Release the brakes when the wheels lock up.
- As soon as the wheels start rolling, apply the brakes fully again. (It can take up to one second for the wheels to start rolling after you release the brakes. If you re-apply the brakes before the wheels start rolling, the vehicle won't straighten out.)

Don't jam on the brakes. Emergency braking does not mean pushing down on the brake pedal as hard as you can. That will only keep the wheels locked up and cause a skid. If the wheels are skidding, you cannot control the vehicle.

Brake failure
Brakes kept in good condition rarely fail. Most hydraulic brake failures occur for one of two reasons:
- Loss of hydraulic pressure.
- Brake fade on long hills.

Loss of hydraulic pressure: When the system won't build up pressure, the brake pedal will feel spongy or go to the floor. Here are some things you can do:
- Downshift. Putting the vehicle into a lower gear will help to slow the vehicle.
- Pump the brakes. Sometimes pumping the brake pedal will generate enough hydraulic pressure to stop the vehicle.
- Use the parking brake. The parking or emergency brake is separate from the hydraulic brake system. Therefore, it can be used to slow the vehicle. However, be sure to press the release button or pull the release lever at the same time you use the emergency brake so you can adjust the brake pressure and keep the wheels from locking up.
- Find an escape route. While slowing the vehicle, look for an escape route--an open field, side street, or escape ramp. Turning uphill is a good way to slow and stop the vehicle. Make sure the vehicle does not start rolling backward after you stop. Put it in low gear, apply the parking brake, and, if necessary, roll back into some obstacle that will stop the vehicle.

Brake failure on downgrades: Going slow enough and braking properly will almost always prevent brake failure on long downgrades. Once the brakes have failed, however, you are going to have to look outside your vehicle for something to stop it. Your best hope is an escape ramp. If there is one available, there will be signs letting you know where each location is. Ramps are usually located a few miles from the top of the downgrade. Every year, hundreds of drivers avoid injury by using escape ramps. Some escape ramps use soft gravel that resists the motion of the vehicle and brings it to a stop. Others turn uphill, using the hill to stop the vehicle and soft gravel to hold it in place. Any driver who loses brakes going downhill should use an escape ramp if it's available. If you don't use it, your chances of having a serious crash may be much greater. If no escape ramp is available, take the least hazardous escape route you can--such as an open field or a side road that flattens out or turns uphill. Make the move as soon as you know your brakes don't work. The longer you wait, the faster the vehicle will go, and the harder it will be to stop.

Tire failure

Quickly recognizing you have a tire failure will let you give you more time to react. Having just a few extra seconds to remember what it is you're supposed to do can help you. The major signs of tire failure are:
- The loud "bang" of a blowout is an easily recognizable sign. It can take a few seconds for your vehicle to react. You might even think it was another vehicle. Any time you hear a tire blow, it would be safest to assume it is yours. Always check.
- Vibration. If the vehicle thumps or vibrates heavily, it may be a sign that one of the tires has gone flat. With a rear tire, that may be the only sign you get.
- Feel. If the steering feels "heavy," it is probably a sign that one of the front tires has failed. Sometimes, failure of a rear tire will cause the vehicle to slide back and forth or "fishtail." However, dual rear tires usually prevent this.

Respond to tire failure. When a tire fails, your vehicle is in danger. You must immediately:
- Hold the steering wheel firmly. If a front tire fails, it can twist the steering wheel out of your hand. The only way to prevent this is to keep a firm grip on the steering wheel with both hands at all times.
- Stay off the brake. It's natural to want to brake in an emergency. However, braking when a tire has failed could cause loss of control. Unless you're about to run into something, stay off the brake until the vehicle has slowed down. Then brake very gently, pull off the road, and stop.
- Check the tires. After you've come to a stop, get out and check all the tires. Do this even if the vehicle seems to be handling all right. If one of your dual tires goes, the only way you may know it is by getting out and looking at it.

Steering to avoid crashing

- Stopping is not always the safest thing to do in an emergency. When you don't have enough room to stop, you may have to steer away from what's ahead. Remember, you can almost always turn to miss an obstacle more quickly than you can stop. (However, top-heavy vehicles and tractors with multiple trailers may flip over.)
- Keep both hands on the steering wheel. In order to turn quickly, you must have a firm grip on the steering wheel with both hands. The best way to have both hands on the wheel, if there is an emergency, is to keep them there all the time.
- Do not apply the brakes while you are turning. This could cause your wheels to lock and you could skid out of control.
- Do not turn any more than needed to clear whatever is in your way. The more sharply you turn, the greater the chances of a skid or rollover.
- Be prepared to "countersteer," that is, to turn the wheel back in the other direction, once you've passed whatever was in your path. Unless you are prepared to countersteer, you won't be able to do it quickly enough. You should think of emergency steering and countersteering as two parts of one driving action.

- If an oncoming driver has drifted into your lane, a move to your right is best. If that driver realizes what has happened, the natural response will be to return to his or her own lane.
- If something is blocking your path, the best direction to steer will depend on the situation. You must be prepared for anything.

In some emergencies, you may have to drive off the road. It may be less risky than facing a collision with another vehicle. Most shoulders are strong enough to support the weight of a large vehicle and, therefore, offer an available escape route. Here are some guidelines, if you do leave the road.
- Avoid braking. If possible, avoid using the brakes until your speed has dropped to about 20 mph. Then brake very gently to avoid skidding on a loose surface.
- Keep one set of wheels on the pavement, if possible. This helps to maintain control.
- Stay on the shoulder. If the shoulder is clear, stay on it until your vehicle has come to a stop. Signal and check your mirrors before pulling back onto the road.

Returning to the road

If you are forced to return to the road before you can stop, use the following procedure:
- Hold the wheel tightly and turn sharply enough to get right back on the road safely.
- Don't try to edge gradually back on the road. If you do, your tires might grab unexpectedly and you could lose control.
- When both front tires are on the paved surface, countersteer immediately. The two turns should be made as a single "steer-countersteer" move.

Skid control and recovery

A skid happens whenever the tires lose their grip on the road. This is caused in one of four ways:
- Over-braking. Braking too hard and locking up the wheels. Skids also can occur when using the speed retarder when the road is slippery.
- Over-steering. Turning the wheels more sharply than the vehicle can turn.
- Over-acceleration. Supplying too much power to the drive wheels, causing them to spin.
- Driving too fast. Most serious skids result from driving too fast for road conditions. Drivers who adjust their driving to conditions don't over-accelerate and don't have to over-brake or over-steer from too much speed.

Drive-wheel skids

By far the most common skid is one in which the rear wheels lose traction through excessive braking or acceleration. Skids caused by acceleration usually happen on ice or snow. Taking your foot off the accelerator can easily stop them. (If it is very slippery, push the clutch in. Otherwise, the engine can keep the wheels from rolling freely and regaining traction.) Rear wheel braking skids occur when the rear drive wheels lock. Because locked wheels have less traction than rolling wheels, the rear wheels usually slide sideways in an attempt to "catch up" with the front wheels. In a bus or straight truck, the vehicle will slide sideways in a "spin out." With vehicles towing trailers, a drive-wheel skid can let the trailer push the towing vehicle sideways, causing a sudden jackknife.

Hazardous Conditions

Driving becomes hazardous when visibility is reduced, or when the road surface is covered with rain, snow or ice. Slow down and increase your following distance.

Night driving

You are at greater risk when you drive at night. Drivers can't see hazards as quickly as in daylight, so they have less time to respond. Drivers caught by surprise are less able to avoid a crash. The problems of night driving involve the driver, the roadway, and the vehicle.

Driver
People can't see as sharply at night or in dim light. Also, their eyes need time to adjust to seeing in dim light. Most people have noticed this when walking into a dark movie theater.
- Drivers can be blinded for a short time by bright light. It takes time to recover from this blindness. Older drivers are especially bothered by glare. Most people have been temporarily blinded by camera flash units or by the high beams of an oncoming vehicle. It can take several seconds to recover from glare. Even two seconds of glare blindness can be dangerous. A vehicle going 55 mph will travel more than half the distance of a football field during that time. Don't look directly at bright lights when driving. Look at the right side of the road. Watch the sidelines when someone coming toward you has very bright lights on.
- Fatigue (being tired) and lack of alertness are bigger problems at night. The body's need for sleep is beyond a person's control. Most people are less alert at night, especially after midnight. This is particularly true if you have been driving for a long time. Drivers may not see hazards as soon, or react as quickly, so the chance of a crash is greater.
- If you are sleepy, the only safe cure is to get off the road and get some sleep. If you don't, you risk your life and the lives of others.

Roadway
- Poor lighting. In the daytime there is usually enough light to see well. This is not true at night. Some areas may have bright street lights, but many areas will have poor lighting. On most roads you will probably have to depend entirely on your headlights. Less light means you will not be able to see hazards as well as in daytime. Road users who do not have lights are hard to see. There are many accidents at night involving pedestrians, joggers, bicyclists, and animals.
- Even when there are lights, the road scene can be confusing. Traffic signals and hazards can be hard to see against a background of signs, shop windows, and other lights. Drive slower when lighting is poor or confusing. Drive slowly enough to be sure you can stop in the distance you can see ahead.
- Drunk drivers. Drunk drivers and drivers under the influence of drugs are a hazard to themselves and to you. Be especially alert around the closing times for bars and taverns. Watch for drivers who have trouble staying in their lane or maintaining speed, who stop without reason, or show other signs of being under the influence of alcohol or drugs.

<u>Vehicle</u>

At night, you must depend a lot on your headlights functioning to see and be seen by other motorists. Your sight is still limited at night, even with the help of your headlights. You need to make necessary adjustments for these limitations.

- Make sure you aren't going faster than it would take to stop within the distance that you can see ahead of you. With your low beams, you can see ahead about 250 feet. With your high beams, you can see ahead between 300 and 500 feet. These are approximations of course. It will vary with each driver. You should make sure you can stop between the approximate distances by adjusting your speed accordingly. This will also vary by the size of the load you are carrying and road conditions. Take everything into account when driving at night.
- Make sure that your headlights are clean and adjusted properly. Dirty headlights do not provide the same amount of light that clean ones do. Dirty headlights defeat their purpose. It makes it much harder for you to see and for others to see you. Proper headlight maintenance is very important.
- Be sure that all lights and reflectors are clean and working so that other drivers can see you. A thorough truck wash should keep you good to go for a while. You just have to continue to monitor everything to stay safe. Clean windows and lights are very important when it comes to driving in any condition. The lights you want to check include:
  - Headlights (high and low beams)
  - Tail lights
  - Turn signals
  - Brake lights
  - Marker lights
  - Clearance lights
  - Identification lights

You should be able to stop within the distance that you can see ahead.

With low beams you can see 250 feet ahead

With high beams you can see 300 to 500 feet ahead

Fog

Fog reflects light and can reflect your own headlights back ████████████████ w beams. Look for road edge markings to guide you. Even light fog r██████████████████ dge distances. If possible, pull off the road and wait until the fo█████████████████ e sure to:

- Obey all fog-related warning signs.
- Reduce you speed.
- Turn on all your lights.
- Use only your low beams.
- Be prepared for sudden stops.

Cold weather driving

<u>Vehicle checks</u>

While performing your pre-trip inspection, you will want to pay close attention to a list of things. First, be sure that the following systems are working properly and that you are confident you know how to use them before operating the vehicle.

- Defrosting and heating equipment: Make sure the defrosters work. They are needed for safe driving. Make sure the heater is working, and that you know how to operate it. If you use other heaters and expect to need them (e.g., mirror heaters, battery box heaters, fuel tank heaters), check their operation.

- Lights and reflectors: Make sure the lights and reflectors are clean. Lights and reflectors are especially important during bad weather. Check from time to time during bad weather to make sure they are clean and working properly.
- Windows and mirrors: Remove any ice, snow, etc., from the windshield, windows, and mirrors before starting. Use a windshield scraper, snow brush, and windshield defroster as necessary. Hand Holds, Steps, and Deck Plates. Remove all ice and snow from hand holds, steps, and deck plates. This will reduce the danger of slipping.
- Radiator shutters and winterfront: Remove ice from the radiator shutters. Make sure the winterfront is not closed too tightly. If the shutters freeze shut or the winterfront is closed too much, the engine may overheat and stop.
- Exhaust system: Exhaust system leaks are especially dangerous when cab ventilation may be poor (windows rolled up, etc.). Loose connections could permit poisonous carbon monoxide to leak into your vehicle. Carbon monoxide gas will cause you to be sleepy. In large enough amounts it can kill you. Check the exhaust system for loose parts and for sounds and signs of leaks.
- Coolant level and antifreeze amount: Make sure the cooling system is full and there is enough antifreeze in the system to protect against freezing. This can be checked with a special coolant tester.
- Wipers and washers: Make sure the windshield wiper blades are in good condition. Make sure the wiper blades press against the window hard enough to wipe the windshield clean, otherwise they may not sweep off snow properly. Make sure the windshield washer works and there is washing fluid in the washer reservoir.
- Tires: Make sure you have enough tread on your tires. The drive tires must provide traction to push the rig over wet pavement and through snow. The steering tires must have traction to steer the vehicle. Enough tread is especially important in winter conditions. You must have at least 4/32 inch tread depth in every major groove on front tires and at least 2/32 inch on other tires. More would be better. Use a gauge to determine if you have enough tread for safe driving.
- Tire chains: You may find yourself in conditions where you can't drive without chains, even to get to a place of safety. Carry the right number of chains and extra cross-links. Make sure they will fit your drive tires. Check the chains for broken hooks, worn or broken cross-links, and bent or broken side chains. Learn how to put the chains on before you need to do it in snow and ice.

Driving tips
- Drive slowly and smoothly on slippery roads. If it is very slippery, you shouldn't drive at all. Stop at the first safe place.
- Adjust turning and braking to conditions. Make turns as gently as possible. Do not brake any harder than necessary, and don't use the engine brake or speed retarder. (They can cause the driving wheels to skid on slippery surfaces.)
- Adjust speed to conditions. Don't pass slower vehicles unless necessary. Go slowly and watch far enough ahead to keep a steady speed. Avoid having to slow down and speed up. Take curves at slower speeds and don't brake while in curves. Be aware that as the temperature rises to the point where ice begins to melt, the road becomes even more slippery. Slow down more.
- Adjust space to conditions. Don't drive alongside other vehicles. Keep a longer following distance. When you see a traffic jam ahead, slow down or stop to wait for it to clear. Try hard to anticipate stops early and slow down gradually. Watch for snowplows, as well as salt and sand trucks, and give them plenty of room.

Wet brakes

When driving in heavy rain or deep standing water, your brakes will get wet. Water in the brakes can cause the brakes to be weak, to apply unevenly, or to grab. This can cause lack of braking power, wheel lockups, pulling to one side or the other, and jackknife if you pull a trailer. Avoid driving through deep puddles or flowing water if possible. If not, you should:

- Slow down and place transmission in a low gear.
- Gently put on the brakes. This presses linings against brake drums or discs and keeps mud, silt, sand, and water from getting in.
- Increase engine rpm and cross the water while keeping light pressure on the brakes.
- When out of the water, maintain light pressure on the brakes for a short distance to heat them up and dry them out.
- Make a test stop when safe to do so. Check behind to make sure no one is following, then apply the brakes to be sure they work well. If not, dry them out further as described above. (CAUTION: Do not apply too much brake pressure and accelerator at the same time, or you can overheat brake drums and linings.)

Hot weather driving

Vehicle checks

Do a normal pre-trip inspection, but pay special attention to the following items.

- Tires: Check the tire mounting and air pressure. Inspect the tires every two hours or every 100 miles when driving in very hot weather. Air pressure increases with temperature. Do not let air out or the pressure will be too low when the tires cool off. If a tire is too hot to touch, remain stopped until the tire cools off. Otherwise the tire may blow out or catch fire.
- Engine oil: The engine oil helps keep the engine cool, as well as lubricating it. Make sure there is enough engine oil. If you have an oil temperature gauge, make sure the temperature is within the proper range while you are driving.
- Engine coolant: Before starting out, make sure the engine cooling system has enough water and antifreeze according to the engine manufacturer's directions. (Antifreeze helps the engine under hot conditions as well as cold conditions.) When driving, check the water temperature or coolant temperature gauge from time to time. Make sure that it remains in the normal range. If the gauge goes above the highest safe temperature, there may be something wrong that could lead to engine failure and possibly fire. Stop driving as soon as safely possible and try to find out what is wrong. Some vehicles have sight glasses, see-through coolant overflow containers, or coolant recovery containers. These permit you to check the coolant level while the engine is hot. If the container is not part of the pressurized system, the cap can be safely removed and coolant added even when the engine is at operating temperature. Never remove the radiator cap or any part of the pressurized system until the system has cooled. Steam and boiling water can spray under pressure and cause severe burns. If you can touch the radiator cap with your bare hand, it is probably cool enough to open. If coolant has to be added to a system without a recovery tank or overflow tank, follow these steps:
  - Shut engine off.
  - Wait until engine has cooled.
  - Protect hands (use gloves or a thick cloth).
  - Turn radiator cap slowly to the first stop, which releases the pressure seal. • Step back while pressure is released from cooling system.
  - When all pressure has been released, press down on the cap and turn it further to remove it.

- o Visually check level of coolant and add more coolant if necessary.
- o Replace cap and turn all the way to the closed position.
- Engine belts: Learn how to check v-belt tightness on your vehicle by pressing on the belts. Loose belts will not turn the water pump and/or fan properly. This will result in overheating. Also, check belts for cracking or other signs of wear.
- Hoses: Make sure coolant hoses are in good condition. A broken hose while driving can lead to engine failure and even fire.

<u>Driving tips</u>
Watch for bleeding tar. Tar in the road pavement frequently rises to the surface in very hot weather. Spots where tar "bleeds" to the surface are very slippery. Go slowly enough to prevent overheating. High speeds create more heat for tires and the engine. In desert conditions the heat may build up to the point where it is dangerous. The heat will increase chances of tire failure or even fire, and engine failure.

Mountain driving

In mountain driving, gravity plays a major role. On any upgrade, gravity slows you down. The steeper the grade, the longer the grade, and/or the heavier the load--the more you will have to use lower gears to climb hills or mountains. In coming down long, steep downgrades, gravity causes the speed of your vehicle to increase. You must select an appropriate safe speed, then use a low gear, and proper braking techniques. You should plan ahead and obtain information about any long, steep grades along your planned route of travel. If possible, talk to other drivers who are familiar with the grades to find out what speeds are safe. You must go slowly enough so your brakes can hold you back without getting too hot. If the brakes become too hot, they may start to "fade." This means you have to apply them harder and harder to get the same stopping power. If you continue to use the brakes hard, they can keep fading until you cannot slow down or stop at all.

Safe speed

Your most important consideration is to select a speed that is not too fast for the:
- Total weight of the vehicle and cargo.
- Length of the grade.
- Steepness of the grade.
- Road conditions.
- Weather
- If a speed limit is posted, or there is a sign indicating "Maximum Safe Speed," never exceed the speed shown. Also, look for and heed warning signs indicating the length and steepness of the grade.
- You must use the braking effect of the engine as the principal way of controlling your speed. The braking effect of the engine is greatest when it is near the governed RPMs and the transmission is in the lower gears.
- Save your brakes so you will be able to slow or stop as required by road and traffic conditions.
- Shift the transmission to a low gear before starting down the grade. Do not try to downshift after your speed has already built up. You will not be able to shift into a lower gear. You may not even be able to get back into any gear and all engine braking effect will be lost. Forcing an automatic transmission into a lower gear at high speed could damage the transmission and also lead to loss of all engine braking effect.

- Use the proper braking technique. Use your brakes on a long, steep downgrade plus the braking power of your engine. When your vehicle is in the proper low gear, use this braking technique:
- Know where the escape ramps are located on your route. Escape ramps have been built on many steep downgrades. They are made to stop runaway vehicles without injuring drivers and passengers. Escape ramps use a long bed of loose soft material to slow runaway vehicles. Use them if you lose your brakes.

Railroad crossing

At many highway-rail grade crossings, the crossbuck sign has flashing red lights and bells. When the lights begin to flash, stop! A train is approaching. You are required to yield the right- of-way to the train. If there is more than one track, make sure all tracks are clear before crossing. Many railroad-highway crossings also have gates with flashing red lights and bells. Stop when the lights begin to flash and before the gate lowers across the road lane. Remain stopped until the gates go up and the lights have stopped flashing. Proceed when it is safe. Never attempt to race a train to a crossing. It is extremely difficult to judge the speed of an approaching train.

- Speed must be reduced in accordance with your ability to see approaching trains in any direction, and speed must be held to a point which will permit you to stop short of the tracks in case a stop is necessary.
- Because of noise inside your vehicle, you cannot expect to hear the train horn until the train is dangerously close to the crossing.
- You should not rely solely upon the presence of warning signals, gates, or flagmen to warn of the approach of trains.
- Double tracks require a double check.
- Remember that a train on one track may hide a train on the other track. Look both ways before crossing. After one train has cleared a crossing, be sure no other trains are near before starting across the tracks.
- Vehicles that have low ground clearance, such as drop frame trailers and car carriers can cause your vehicle to hang up on railroad crossings with steep approaches. If you get hung up on a railroad crossing, call 9-1-1 immediately so that the scheduled trains can be notified to stop.
- Be sure you can get all the way across the tracks before you begin to cross.
- Do not shift gears when crossing railroad tracks.
- A full stop is required at grade crossings whenever:
  o The nature of the cargo makes a stop mandatory under state or federal regulations.
  o Such a stop is otherwise required by law.
- When stopping be sure to:
  o Check for traffic behind you while stopping gradually. Use a pullout lane, if available.
  o Turn on your four-way emergency flashers.

Equipment failures

Brake failures
Brakes kept in good condition rarely fail. Most hydraulic brake failures occur for one of two reasons:
- Loss of hydraulic pressure
- Brake fade on long hills

When the system won't build up pressure, the brake pedal will feel spongy or go to the floor. Here are some things you can do:

- Downshift. Putting the vehicle into a lower gear will help to slow the vehicle.
- Pump the brakes. Sometimes pumping the brake pedal will generate enough hydraulic pressure to stop the vehicle.

Airbrake fading or failure

Excessive use of the service brakes results in overheating and leads to brake fade. Brake fade results from excessive heat causing chemical changes in the brake lining, which reduce friction, and also causing expansion of the brake drums. As the overheated drums expand, the brake shoes and linings have to move farther to contact the drums, and the force of this contact is reduced. Continued overuse may increase brake fade until the vehicle cannot be slowed down or stopped. Brake fade is also affected by adjustment. To safely control a vehicle, every brake must do its share of the work. Brakes out of adjustment will stop doing their share before those that are in adjustment. The other brakes can then overheat and fade, and there will not be enough braking available to control the vehicle(s). Brakes can get out of adjustment quickly, especially when they are hot. Therefore, check brake adjustment often

Tire failure

The sooner that you realize that a tire has failed, the more time you will have to react to the situation. The recognizable signs of tire failure are:

- Sound. You may hear a loud bang that often accompanies a blowout. However, you may mistake the noise for another vehicle as yours will not have an immediate effect on your driving. It is best to always assume it was one of yours and to use your mirrors to check.
- Vibration. If your vehicle vibrates, you may have a tire failure. With a rear tire, this may be the only sign you get as tandem wheels often compensate for the failed tire.
- Feel. If it becomes harder than usual to control your steering, one of the front tires has probably failed.

If a tire fails, take the following steps:

- Maintain a solid grip on the steering wheel. If a front tire fails, it can cause the wheel to twist out of your hands. Keep both hands on the wheel at all times.
- Stay off the brakes. If you brake during a tire failure, it could cause you to lose control of the vehicle. Unless it is necessary for the safety of you or fellow drivers, stay off the brake until the vehicle has slowed down on its own (engine brakes can help this). Then, brake gently and pull off the road.
- Check the tires even if the vehicle seems to be handling normally. Many times you won't know that a dual tire is flat unless you look at it.

Crashes

As a professional driver, if you are in a crash and not seriously hurt; you need to take three steps to prevent further damage or injury to yourself or others:

- Protect the scene (keep people away):
  - Protect the area to prevent another crash. This is the first thing you need to do.
  - If your vehicle is involved in the crash, try to move it out of the roadway. This will help prevent additional crashes.
  - If you are stopping to help at the scene of a crash, park far away from the crash. The area around the crash will be needed by emergency vehicles.

- o Put on your flashers.
  - o Set out reflective triangles to warn other traffic. Make sure that other drivers will see them in time to avoid another crash by following the same distance rules as if you were stalled on the side of the road.
- Notify the authorities as soon as possible (inform them of your cargo if hazardous). If you have a CB radio or cell phone, put out a call over the emergency channel or dial 911 before leaving your vehicle. If you have no way to contact authorities, wait until the crash scene has been protected, then call or send someone to call the police. Remember to determine where you are before contacting anyone so you can provide an accurate location of the crash.
- Care for the injured (never move them unless they are able to move themselves). If a qualified person is helping the injured, stay out of their way unless you are asked to assist. Otherwise, make every effort to help anyone who could be injured. Don't move a severely injured person unless there is a danger of fire or passing traffic makes it necessary. Stop heavy bleeding by applying direct pressure to the wound. Keep the injured person warm.

Fires

You might have to control minor truck fires on the road. However, unless you have the training and equipment to do so safely, don't fight hazardous materials fires. Dealing with hazardous materials fires requires special training and protective gear. When you discover a fire, call for help. You may use the fire extinguisher to keep minor truck fires from spreading to cargo before firefighters arrive. Feel trailer doors to see if they are hot before opening them. If hot, you may have a cargo fire and should not open the doors. Opening doors lets air in and may make the fire flare up. Without air, many fires only smolder until firemen arrive, doing less damage. If your cargo is already on fire, it is not safe to fight the fire. Keep the shipping papers with you to give to emergency personnel as soon as they arrive. Warn other people of the danger and keep them away. If you discover a cargo leak, identify the hazardous materials leaking by using shipping papers, labels, or package location.

Do not touch any leaking material--many people injure themselves by touching hazardous materials. Do not try to identify the material or find the source of a leak by smell. Toxic gases can destroy your sense of smell and can injure or kill you even if they don't smell. Never eat, drink, or smoke around a leak or spill. If hazardous materials are spilling from your vehicle, do not move it any more than safety requires. You may move off the road and away from places where people gather, if doing so serves safety. Only move your vehicle if you can do so without danger to yourself or others.

Hazardous materials

Rules for all commercial drivers

Hazardous materials are products that pose a risk to health, safety, and property during transportation. The term often is shortened to HAZMAT, which you may see on road signs, or to HM in government regulations. Hazardous materials include explosives, various types of gas, solids, flammable and combustible liquid, and other materials. Because of the risks involved and the potential consequences these risks impose, all levels of government regulate the handling of hazardous materials. The Hazardous Materials Regulations (HMR) is found in parts 100 - 185 of title 49 of the Code of Federal Regulations. The common reference for these regulations is 49 CFR 100 – 185. The table below lists 9 hazard classes:

Class	Division	Name of Class or Division	Example
1	1.1	Explosives (Mass	Dynamite
	1.2	Detonations)	Ammunition for Cannons
	1.3	Projection Hazards	Display Fireworks
	1.4	Mass Fire Hazards	Small Arms Ammunition
	1.5	Minor Hazards	Blasting Agents
	1.6	Very Insensitive	Explosive Devices
		Extremely Insensitive	
2	2.1	Flammable Gases	Propane
	2.2	Non-Flammable Gases	Helium
	2.3	Poisonous/Toxic Gases	Fluorine, Compressed
3	---	Flammable Liquids	Gasoline, Diesel Fuel
4	4.1	Flammable Solids	Ammonium Picrate, Wetted White
	4.2	Spontaneous Combustible	Phosphorus
	4.3	Dangerous When Wet	Sodium
5	5.1	Oxidizers	Ammonium Nitrate
	5.2	Organic Peroxides	Methyl Ethyl Ketone Peroxide
6	6.1	Poison (Toxic Material)	Potassium Cyanide
	6.2	Infectious Substances	Anthrax Virus
7	---	Radioactive	Uranium
8	---	Corrosives	Battery Fluid
9	---	Miscellaneous Hazardous Materials	Polychlorinated Biphenyls (PCB)
None	---	ORM-D (Other Regulated Material-Domestic)	Food Flavorings, Medicines, Cleaning Compounds, and Other Consumer Commodities
None	---	Combustible Liquids	Fuel Oil

You must follow the rules for transporting hazardous materials. These rules ensure safe drivers and equipment. They also tell you how to contain the product and how to communicate its risk. The regulations require vehicles transporting certain types or quantities of hazardous materials to display diamond-shaped, square on point, warning signs called placards. You must have a commercial driver license (CDL) with a hazardous materials endorsement before you drive any size vehicle that is used to transport hazardous material as defined in 49 CFR 383.5. You must pass a written test about the regulations and requirements to get this endorsement.

Containment rules

Transporting hazardous materials can be risky. The regulations are intended to protect you, those around you, and the environment. They tell shippers how to package the materials safely and drivers how to load, transport, and unload the material. These are called "containment rules."

Communicating the risk

To communicate the risk, shippers must warn drivers and others about the material's hazards. The regulations require shippers to put hazard warning labels on packages, provide proper shipping papers, emergency response information, and placards. These steps communicate the hazard to the shipper, the carrier, and the driver. Placards are 10 ¾ inches on each side and are diamond-shaped. Cargo tanks and other bulk packaging display the I.D. number of their contents on placards or orange panels. A placarded vehicle must have at least 4 identical placards. They are placed on the front, rear and both sides of the vehicle. Not all vehicles that carry hazardous materials need placards. The regulations about placards are given in Section 9 of this driver's manual. You can drive a vehicle carrying hazardous materials if it does not require placards. If it requires placards, you may not drive it unless you have a hazardous material endorsement on your commercial driver's license.

Roles in hazardous material transportation

Shipper:
- Sends products from one place to another by truck, rail, vessel, or airplane.
- Uses the hazardous materials regulations to determine the product's:
  - Proper shipping name.
  - Hazard class.
  - Identification number.
  - Packing group.
  - Correct packaging.
  - Correct label and markings.
  - Correct placards.
- Must package, mark, and label the materials; prepare shipping papers; provide emergency response information; and supply placards.
- Certify on the shipping paper that the shipment has been prepared according to the rules (unless you are pulling cargo tanks supplied by you or your employer).

Carrier:
- Takes the shipment from the shipper to its destination.
- Prior to transportation, checks that the shipper correctly described, marked, labeled, and otherwise prepared the shipment for transportation.
- Refuses improper shipments.
- Reports accidents and incidents involving hazardous materials to the proper government agency.

Driver:
- Makes sure the shipper has identified, marked, and labeled the hazardous materials properly.
- Refuses leaking packages and shipments.
- Placards vehicle when loading, if required.
- Safely transports the shipment without delay.
- Follows all special rules about transporting hazardous materials.

- Keeps hazardous material shipping papers and emergency response information in the proper place.

General Knowledge Test

Practice Questions

1. What is the minimum amount of tread depth that your tires should have?
   a. There should be at least four-thirty seconds tread depth in every major groove on the front wheels and at least two-thirty seconds inch tread on all other wheels.
   b. There should be at least one-inch tread depth in every major groove on all wheels.
   c. There should be at least four-thirty seconds inch tread depth in every major groove on all wheels.

2. How do you test hydraulic brakes for a leak?
   a. With the vehicle under way at a low speed, apply firm pressure, stopping the vehicle as quickly as possible.
   b. With the vehicle stopped, push down the brake pedal and do not release for at least five seconds.
   c. With the vehicle stopped, pump the brake pedal three times. Apply firm pressure, and then hold for five seconds.

3. How do you test hydraulic brakes for their stopping action?
   a. Go about five miles per hour. Push the brake pedal firmly.
   b. With the vehicle stopped, pump the brake pedal three times. Apply firm pressure, and then hold for five seconds.
   c. With the vehicle stopped, push the brake pedal firmly, and then hold for five seconds.

4. How does tire pressure affect hydroplaning?
   a. Hydroplaning is not affected by tire pressure.
   b. Hydroplaning is more likely to occur when tire pressure is low.
   c. Hydroplaning is more likely to occur when tires are over inflated.

5. What is the best way to use the brake pedal on a steep downhill grade?
   a. Use a heavy pressure repeatedly.
   b. Avoid using the brakes.
   c. Shift to a lower gear before starting downgrade and use a light, steady pressure on the brake pedal.

6. What is a good rule as to the speed you should go when driving at night?
   a. You should keep your speed slow enough to stop within the range of your headlights.
   b. You do not have to be able to stop within the distance that you can see.
   c. You should never drive so fast as to require your high beams.

7. How many times more distance does it take to stop whenever you double your speed?
   a. Twice as much distance.
   b. Three times as much distance.
   c. Four times as much distance.

8. In checking tires what are some problems that you should look for?
    a. Too much or too little specification information on the sidewalls.
    b. Bad wear, cuts or other damage, tread separation, cut or cracked valve stems. Dual tires that come in contact, mismatched sizes, radial and bias-ply tires used together.
    c. Regrooved, recapped, or retreaded tires on the drive wheels.

9. What are some steering system defects to look for?
    a. Missing nuts, bolts, cotter keys or other parts; bent, loose or broken parts.
    b. Steering wheel play of two degrees.
    c. Steering wheel play of five degrees.

10. What are some defects to look for in the suspension system?
    a. Spring hangers that allow movement of the axle from the proper position; cracked or broken spring hangers; spring hangers or other axle positioning parts that are cracked damaged, or missing.
    b. Oil leaks in the frame or fifth wheel assembly.
    c. Oil leaks in the brake drums.

11. In holding a steering wheel what is the proper way to place your hands?
    a. Loosely with at least one hand on the wheel.
    b. One hand at the top of the wheel and one hand at the bottom of the wheel. In terms of the clock your hands should be at six o'clock and twelve o'clock.
    c. Firmly with both hands and your hands should be on opposite sides of the wheel. In terms of the clock, your hands should be at three o'clock and nine o'clock.

12. What are some things to do when you are backing your vehicle?
    a. First, look at your path. Second, back slowly. Third, back, straight back.
    b. Insist on having a helper to guide you.
    c. Back and turn from the right whenever possible.

13. What is meant by double clutching?
    a. Pushing down on the clutch pedal four times each time you shift gears.
    b. Shifting without using the clutch.
    c. Release the accelerator, push down on the clutch pedal and shift to neutral; then release the clutch pedal; then let the engine and gears slow down to the RPMs required for the nest gear; then push in the clutch pedal and shift to the higher gear.

14. What are two factors in knowing when to shift?
    a. Using transmission speed and clutch stroke.
    b. Using engine speed and road speed.
    c. Using road speed and "feel" of the road.

15. What is one way of knowing when you have the right engine speed and road speed to shift gears?
    a. When the engine is lugging.
    b. By shifting whenever you notice heavy smoke coming from the exhaust stack.
    c. Using the sound of the engine to know when to shift.

16. What is true about downshifting <u>before</u> you reach a long downhill grade?
    a. It helps prevent the brakes from overheating and losing their braking power.
    b. It puts an extra burden on the brake system.
    c. Starting on a downhill grade in low gear increases the chance of the truck picking up speed and going out of control.

17. When should you downshift for a curve?
    a. Slow down to a safe speed and downshift to the proper gear before entering the curve.
    b. Slow down to a safe speed and downshift to the proper gear upon entering the curve.
    c. Slow down to a safe speed and downshift after entering the curve.

18. What is the purpose of brake retarders?
    a. To help slow down the vehicle and to reduce brake wear.
    b. To provide more traction on a slippery surface and enable a vehicle to go faster.
    c. To reduce brake wear and to reduce noise.

19. Should you turn the retarder off when the road is wet, icy, or snow covered?
    a. No, because you need more braking power then.
    b. No, because the engine retarder will have no effect on traction.
    c. Yes, whenever your drive wheels have poor traction the retarder may cause a skid.

20. How far ahead should you look while driving?
    a. 100 feet
    b. Four seconds
    c. 12 to 15 seconds

21. What is a good reason for knowing what the traffic is doing on all sides of you?
    a. Stopping or changing lanes can take time and distance and you need to have room to make these moves safely.
    b. It is always necessary to know when you can make a U-turn.
    c. You need to eliminate all blind spots around you.

22. Should you <u>always</u> be looking into the distance ahead?
    a. Yes, You should be prepared for all problems ahead.
    b. No, you should shift your attention back and forth, near and far.
    c. Yes, by concentrating on the vehicle directly ahead you will be prepared for all emergencies.

23. What is a problem that you can have when using your mirrors?
    a. They never remain in the positions you have placed them.
    b. They are of no help when you are changing lanes.
    c. There are blind spots that your mirrors cannot show you.

24. Where do you place the three reflector triangles if you have to park on the side of a level, straight two-lane road?
    a. Place one within 10 feet of the rear of the vehicle, one about 100 feet to the rear and one about 100 feet from the front of the vehicle.
    b. Place one within 100 feet of the front of the vehicle, one 500 feet from the front of the vehicle and one about 100 feet from the rear of the vehicle.
    c. Place one within 10 feet of the front of the vehicle, one about 100 feet to the front and one about 500 feet to the rear of the vehicle.

25. Where do you place the three reflector triangles if you have to park on the side of a level highway with one-way traffic such as a divided highway?
 a. Place them to the rear of the vehicle; one within 10 feet, one within 100 feet and the other one 200 feet.
 b. Place all of them in front of the vehicle up to 500 feet.
 c. Place two in front of the vehicle at 10 feet and at 100 feet and place one to the rear of the vehicle.

26. What are three factors that add up to total stopping distance with hydraulic-brakes?
 a. Brake lag distance, pedal engaging distance, rolling distance.
 b. Reaction distance, application distance, braking distance.
 c. Perception distance, reaction distance, braking distance.

27. Why do empty trucks usually require greater stopping distance than loaded trucks?
 a. An empty truck has less traction.
 b. An empty truck has more forward momentum.
 c. An empty truck has less brakes.

28. What should you do if your vehicle hydroplanes?
 a. Let up on the clutch.
 b. Release the accelerator and push in the clutch.
 c. Push down on the accelerator releasing the clutch.

29. How long does it take for the average driver to bring a heavy vehicle to a stop when driving 55 miles per hour on dry pavement?
 a. About 100 feet... about 2 seconds
 b. About 200 feet... about 4 seconds.
 c. About 300 feet... about 6 seconds.

30. You are driving a vehicle with a light load. Traffic is moving at 35 miles per hour in a 55 mile per hour zone. What is most likely the safest speed for your vehicle in this situation?
 a. 55 miles per hour
 b. 35 miles per hour
 c. 45 miles per hour

31. When driving how much space should you try to keep in front of you?
 a. One second for each 15 feet of your vehicle length at speeds below 40 miles per hour.
 b. Over 40 miles per hour at least one second for each 10 feet of your vehicle length plus one extra second.
 c. With a forty-foot vehicle leave 5 seconds between you and the vehicle ahead when going below 40 miles per hour.

32. What are some things to do if you are being tailgated?
 a. Avoid quick changes of speed or direction.
 b. Try to reduce your following distance.
 c. Speed up, and flash your taillights on and off.

33. What is one reason that you can never assure that you're safe by reading the heights posted at bridges and overpasses?
    a. Repaving or packed snow may have decreased the clearances since the heights were posted.
    b. The weight of a cargo van can change its height with an empty van being lighter or lower.
    c. Some roads can cause your vehicle to tilt.

34. You wish to turn right from a two-lane, two-way street to another. Your vehicle is so long that you must swing wide to make the turn. How should the turn be made?
    a. Start turning wide before you enter the turn.
    b. You may allow your rear trailer wheels to climb over the curb.
    c. Turn wide as you complete the turn.

35. With a large vehicle, if you are turning left, which lane should you use if there are two left turn lanes?
    a. Use either lane.
    b. Use the right hand lane.
    c. Use the left hand lane

36. Since it is difficult to look directly at bright lights when driving, where can you look to avoid the glare of oncoming traffic?
    a. Close your eyes momentarily.
    b. Try to look at the centerline of the highway, watching for the dotted line.
    c. Try to look at the right side of the road, watching the sidelines.

37. What are some items that you <u>must</u> check especially before driving in winter weather?
    a. CB Radio Antenna
    b. Coolant level, windshield washer antifreeze.
    c. AM-FM Radio

38. How often should you check your tires when driving in very hot weather?
    a. Every 2 hours or every 100 miles.
    b. Every time you stop.
    c. Once each hour.

39. Will "fanning" your brakes, allow them to cool so that they won't overheat on a steep downgrade?
    a. Yes, short heavy application of the brakes will prevent the brakes from overheating.
    b. No, the brake system is not affected by "fanning."
    c. No, brake drums cool very slowly and the brakes may begin to fade and have less stopping power when the pressure is not applied steadily.

40. What are some hazards that are frequently seen on the highway?
    a. Workers, children, inattentive drivers, hurrying drivers, impaired drivers, suicides.
    b. Work zones, accidents.
    c. Road edge drop-offs, crashed airplanes, disabled vehicles.

41. What can you do to lessen the chances of having to make a sudden move to avoid hazards?
    a. Keep your vehicle centered in your lane by watching the white line up close.
    b. Watch far enough ahead so that hazards can be anticipated.
    c. Follow the driver ahead closely and watch his brake lights.

42. In emergencies you may be able to miss an obstacle more quickly than you can stop. What is a characteristic of heavy vehicles when they are turned quickly?
    a. Top-heavy vehicles and tractors with multiple trailers cannot be turned quickly.
    b. Top-heavy vehicles and tractors with multiple trailers will unhook when turned quickly.
    c. Top-heavy vehicles and tractors with multiple trailers may flip over when turned quickly.

43. You are driving on a two-lane road when an oncoming driver drifts into your lane and is heading straight for you. What is one action to take?
    a. Braking while veering to the right when possible.
    b. Quickly turn to the left.
    c. Speed up to maneuver around the oncoming vehicle.

44. In making a quick turn what is a point to remember?
    a. Do not apply the brake when you are turning.
    b. The brakes will prevent skidding in turns.
    c. Do not expect to counter-steer.

45. What is controlled braking?
    a. Brake so that your wheels will stop rolling and bring the vehicle to a quick stop.
    b. Apply your brakes fully and do not release them.
    c. Applying the brakes as hard as you can without locking the wheels.

46. What is the major cause of most serious skids?
    a. Turning too sharply.
    b. Locking up the wheels.
    c. Driving too fast for road conditions.

47. What is the only way to stop a front wheel skid?
    a. Turn harder and brake harder.
    b. Stop turning and brake harder.
    c. Let the vehicle slow down. Stop turning and stop braking so hard.

48. If you think that a tire has blown out, what should you do in stopping?
    a. Hold the steering wheel firmly. Do not touch the brakes until the vehicle has slowed down when you can brake very gently.
    b. Hold the steering wheel firmly. Use hard braking to get off the highway as soon as possible and stop.
    c. Hold the steering wheel loosely. Use hard braking to stop.

49. What is something that you must do when using a fire extinguisher to fight a fire?
    a. Stay downwind.
    b. Aim at the base of the fire.
    c. Aim at the top of the fire.

50. As a driver for what are you responsible regarding your cargo?
    a. Inspecting your cargo, knowing that your cargo is securely tied down or covered, recognizing overloads and poorly balanced loads.
    b. Inspecting your cargo and keeping rainwater from getting under the pallets.
    c. Shifting your cargo at state lines and sliding your fifth wheel.

51. How often should cargo inspections be made?
    a. After every break during driving.
    b. Once each hour.
    c. Every 25 miles.

52. What is important about the center of gravity of a load?
    a. A high center of gravity keeps you from seeing back of your trailers.
    b. A high center of gravity means you are more likely to tip over.
    c. A high center of gravity means you may not clear certain overpasses.

53. What can happen if you don't have enough weight on the steering axle?
    a. This will make the vehicle easier to control in turns.
    b. This can make the vehicle easier to steer straight.
    c. This can make the vehicle harder to steer.

54. What is the minimum distance between tie downs to prevent shifting of cargo?
    a. Every six feet.
    b. Every ten feet.
    c. Every eighteen feet.

55. What is the minimum number of tie downs that you should have?
    a. Two
    b. Four
    c. Six

56. What is the purpose of blocking and bracing?
    a. To keep cargo from sliding, falling and getting out of balance.
    b. To keep containers from getting dirty.
    c. To support the trailer structure.

57. Must you show your logbook to officers?
    a. Yes.
    b. No.
    c. Only after they have read you your rights.

Answer Key

1. A

2. C

3. A

4. B

5. C

6. A

7. C

8. B

9. A

10. A

11. C

12. A

13. C

14. B

15. C

16. A

17. A

18. A

19. C

20. C

21. A

22. B

23. C

24. A

25. A

26. C

27. A

28. B

29. C

30. B

31. B

32. A

33. A

34. C

35. B

36. C

37. B

38. A

39. C

40. B

41. B

42. C

43. A

44. A

45. C

46. C

47. C

48. A

49. B

50. A

51. A

52. B

53. C

54. B

55. A

56. A

57. A

Air Brakes Endorsement

Air brakes

Air brakes use compressed air to make the brakes work. Air brakes are a good and safe way of stopping large and heavy vehicles, but the brakes must be well maintained and used properly. When we discuss air brakes, we are actually discussing three different braking systems. They are:

- Service brake - The service brake system applies and releases the brakes when you use the brake pedal during normal driving.
- Parking brake - The parking brake system applies and releases the parking brakes when you use the parking brake control. There are parking brakes for the truck and the trailer. When connected to a trailer, always set both brakes when parking.
- Emergency brake - The emergency brake system uses parts of the service and parking brake systems to stop the vehicle in a brake system failure.

Air brake system parts

Air compressor: The air compressor pumps air into the air storage tanks (reservoirs). The air compressor is connected to the engine through gears or a v-belt. The compressor may be air cooled or may be cooled by the engine cooling system. It may have its own oil supply or be lubricated by engine oil. If the compressor has its own oil supply, check the oil level before driving.

Air compressor governor: The governor controls when the air compressor will pump air into the air storage tanks. When air tank pressure rises to the "cut-out" level (around 125 pounds per-square-inch or "psi"), the governor stops the compressor from pumping air. When the tank pressure falls to the "cut-in" pressure (around 100 psi), the governor allows the compressor to start pumping again.

Air storage tanks: Air storage tanks are used to hold compressed air. The number and size of air tanks varies among vehicles. The tanks will hold enough air to allow the brakes to be used several times, even if the compressor stops working.

Air tank drains: Compressed air usually has some water and some compressor oil in it, which is bad for the air brake system. For example, the water can freeze in cold weather and cause brake failure. The water and oil tend to collect in the bottom of the air tank. Be sure that you drain the air tanks completely. Each air tank is equipped with a drain valve in the bottom. There are two types:
- Manually operated by turning a quarter turn or by pulling a cable. You must drain the tanks yourself at the end of each day of driving.
- Automatic--the water and oil are automatically expelled. These tanks may be equipped for manual draining as well. Automatic air tanks are available with electric heating devices. These help prevent freezing of the automatic drain in cold weather.

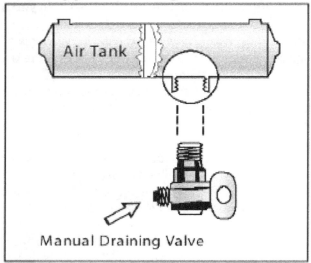

Alcohol evaporator: Some air brake systems have an alcohol evaporator to put alcohol into the air system. This helps to reduce the risk of ice in air brake valves and other parts during cold weather. Ice inside the system can make the brakes stop working. Check the alcohol container and fill up as necessary, every day during cold weather. Daily air tank drainage is still needed to get rid of water and oil. (Unless the system has automatic drain valves.)

Safety valve: A safety relief valve is installed in the first tank the air compressor pumps air to. The safety valve protects the tank and the rest of the system from too much pressure. The valve is usually set to open at 150 psi. If the safety valve releases air, something is wrong. Have the fault fixed by a mechanic.

The brake pedal: You put on the brakes by pushing down the brake pedal. (It is also called the foot valve or treadle valve.) Pushing the pedal down harder applies more air pressure. Letting up on the brake pedal reduces the air pressure and releases the brakes. Releasing the brakes lets some compressed air go out of the system, so the air pressure in the tanks is reduced. It must be made up by the air compressor. Pressing and releasing the pedal unnecessarily can let air out faster than the compressor can replace it. If the pressure gets too low, the brakes won't work.

Foundation brakes: Foundation brakes are used at each wheel. The most common type is the s-cam drum brake.

Brake drums, shoes, and linings: Brake drums are located on each end of the vehicle's axles. The wheels are bolted to the drums. The braking mechanism is inside the drum. To stop, the brake shoes and linings are pushed against the inside of the drum. This causes friction, which slows the vehicle (and creates heat). The heat a drum can take without damage depends on how hard and how long the brakes are used. Too much heat can make the brakes stop working.

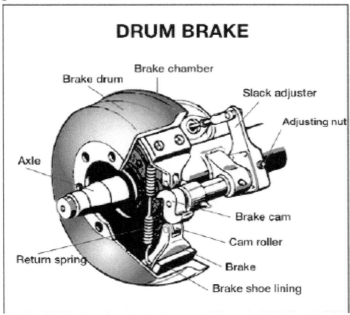

DRUM BRAKE

Supply pressure gauges: All vehicles with air brakes have a pressure gauge connected to the air tank. If the vehicle has a dual air brake system, there will be a gauge for each half of the system. (Or a single gauge with two needles.) Dual systems will be discussed later. These gauges tell you how much pressure is in the air tanks.

Application pressure gauge: This gauge shows you how much air pressure is being applied to the brakes. (This gauge is not on all vehicles.) Increasing application pressure to hold the same speed means the brakes are fading. You should slow down and use a lower gear. The need for increased pressure can also be caused by brakes out of adjustment, air leaks, or mechanical problems.

Low air pressure warning: A low air pressure warning signal is required on vehicles with air brakes. A warning signal you can see must come on before the air pressure in the tanks falls below 60 psi. (Or one half the compressor governor cutout pressure on older vehicles.) The warning is usually a red light. A buzzer may also come on.

Stop light switch: Drivers behind you must be warned when you put your brakes on. The air brake system does this with an electric switch that works by air pressure. The switch turns on the brake lights when you put on the air brakes.

Front brake limiting valve: Some older vehicles (made before 1975) have a front brake limiting valve and a control in the cab. The control is usually marked "normal" and "slippery." When you put the control in the "slippery" position, the limiting valve cuts the "normal" air pressure to the front brakes by half. Limiting valves were used to reduce the chance of the front wheels skidding on slippery surfaces. However, they actually reduce the stopping power of the vehicle. Front wheel braking is good under all conditions. Tests have shown front wheel skids from braking are not likely even on ice. Make sure the control is in the "Normal" position to have normal stopping power. Many vehicles have automatic front wheel limiting valves. They reduce the air to the front brakes except when the brakes are put on very hard (60 psi or more application pressure). These valves cannot be controlled by the driver.

Spring brakes: Many vehicles have automatic front wheel limiting valves. They reduce the air to the front brakes except when the brakes are put on very hard (60 psi or more application pressure). These valves cannot be controlled by the driver. Tractor and straight truck spring brakes will activate fully when air pressure drops to a range between 20 to 45 psi (typically 20 to 30 psi). Do not wait for the brakes to come on automatically. When the low air pressure warning light and buzzer first come on, bring the vehicle to a safe stop right away, while you still have control of the brakes. The braking power of spring brakes depends on the brakes being in adjustment. If the brakes are not adjusted properly, neither the regular brakes nor the emergency/parking brakes will work right.

Parking brake controls: In newer vehicles with air brakes, you put on the parking brakes using a diamond-shaped, yellow, push-pull control knob. You pull the knob out to put the parking brakes (spring brakes) on, and push it in to release them. On older vehicles, the parking brakes may be controlled by a lever. Use the parking brakes whenever you park.
Never push the brake pedal down when the spring brakes are on. If you do, the brakes could be damaged by the combined forces of the springs and the air pressure. Many brake systems are designed in a way that will not allow this to happen. However, not all systems are set up that way, and those that are may not always work.

Modulating control valves: In some vehicles a control handle on the dash board may be used to apply the spring brakes gradually. This is called a modulating valve. It is spring-loaded so you have a feel for the braking action. The more you move the control lever, the harder the spring brakes come on. They work this way so you can control the spring brakes if the service brakes fail. When parking a vehicle with a modulating control valve, move the lever as far as it will go and hold it in place with the locking device.

Dual parking control valves: When main air pressure is lost, the spring brakes come on. Some vehicles, such as buses, have a separate air tank which can be used to release the spring brakes. This is so you can move the vehicle in an emergency. One of the valves is a push-pull type and is used to put on the spring brakes for parking. The other valve is spring loaded in the "out" position. When you push the control in, air from the separate air tank releases the spring brakes so you can move. When you release the button, the spring brakes come on again. There is only enough air in the separate tank to do this a few times. Therefore, plan carefully when moving. Otherwise, you may be stopped in a dangerous location when the separate air supply runs out. Use the parking brakes whenever you park.

Antilock Braking Systems (ABS): Truck tractors with air brakes built on or after March 1, 1997, and other air brakes vehicles, (trucks, buses, trailers, and converter dollies) built on or after March 1, 1998, are required to be equipped with antilock brakes. Many commercial vehicles built before these dates have been voluntarily equipped with ABS. Check the certification label for the date of manufacture to determine if your vehicle is equipped with ABS. ABS is a computerized system that keeps your wheels from locking up during hard brake applications. Vehicles with ABS have yellow malfunction lamps to tell you if something isn't working. Tractors, trucks, and buses will have yellow ABS malfunction lamps on the instrument panel. Trailers will have yellow ABS malfunction lamps on the left side, either on the front or rear corner. Dollies manufactured on or after March 1, 1998 are required to have a lamp on the left side.

On newer vehicles, the malfunction lamp comes on at start-up for a bulb check, and then goes out quickly. On older systems, the lamp could stay on until you are driving over five mph. If the lamp stays on after the bulb check, or goes on once you are under way, you may have lost ABS control at one or more wheels. In the case of towed units manufactured before it was required by the Department of Transportation, it may be difficult to tell if the unit is equipped with ABS. Look under the vehicle for the electronic control unit (ECU) and wheel speed sensor wires coming from the back of the brakes. ABS is an addition to your normal brakes. It does not decrease or increase your normal braking capability. ABS only activates when wheels are about to lock up. ABS does not necessarily shorten your stopping distance, but it does help you keep the vehicle under control during hard braking.

Dual air brake systems

Most heavy-duty vehicles use dual air brake systems for safety. A dual air brake system has two separate air brake systems, which use a single set of brake controls. Each system has its own air tanks, hoses, lines, etc. One system typically operates the regular brakes on the rear axle or axles. The other system operates the regular brakes on the front axle (and possibly one rear axle). Both systems supply air to the trailer (if there is one). The first system is called the "primary" system. The other is called the "secondary" system. Before driving a vehicle with a dual air system, allow time for the air compressor to build up a minimum of 100 psi pressure in both the primary and secondary systems. Watch the primary and secondary air pressure gauges (or needles, if the system has two needles in one gauge). Pay attention to the low air pressure warning light and buzzer. The warning light and buzzer should shut off when air pressure in both systems rises to a value set by the manufacturer. This value must be greater than 60 psi. The warning light and buzzer should come on before the air pressure drops below 60 psi in either system. If this happens while driving, you should stop right away and safely park the vehicle. If one air system is very low on pressure, either the front or the rear brakes will not be operating fully. This means it will take you longer to stop. Bring the vehicle to a safe stop, and have the air brakes system fixed.

Inspecting air brake systems

There are more things to inspect on a vehicle with air brakes than one without them:
- Engine compartment check
  - Check the air compressor drive belt if the compressor is belt driven. Check the condition and tightness of the belt.
- Walk-around inspection
  - Check the manual slack adjusters on the S-Cam brakes.
  - Park on level ground and chock the wheels.
  - Turn off the parking brakes so you can move the slack adjusters.
  - Use gloves and pull hard on each slack adjuster that you can reach.
  - If a slack adjuster moves more than about one inch where the push rod attaches to it, it probably needs adjustment.
  - Adjust it or have it adjusted. Vehicles with too much brake slack can be hard to stop. Out-of-adjustment brakes are the most common problem found in roadside inspections.
  - Check the brake drums (or discs), linings and hoses.
  - Brake drums or discs cannot have cracks longer than half the width of the friction area.
  - Linings (friction material) cannot be loose, soaked with oil or grease. They cannot be dangerously thin.

- o Mechanical parts must be in place and should not be broken or missing.
- o Check the air hoses connected to the brake chambers to make sure they are not cut or worn due to rubbing.
- Check the air brake system.
  - o Checking the air brake system is different from the hydraulic brake check shown in Section 1: General Knowledge.
    - Test the low pressure warning signal.
    - Shut off the engine when you have enough air pressure so that the low pressure warning signal is off.
    - Turn on the electrical power and step on and off the brake pedal to reduce air tank pressure.
    - The low air pressure warning signal must come on before the pressure drops to less than 60 psi in the air tank (or tank with the lowest air pressure in dual air systems).
    - If the warning signal doesn't work, you could lose air pressure without knowing it. This could cause sudden emergency braking. In dual systems, the stopping distance will be increased. Only limited breaking can be done before the spring brakes come on.
  - o Be sure that spring brakes come on automatically.
    - Chock the wheels, release the parking brakes when you have enough air pressure and shut off the engine.
    - Step on and off the brake pedal to reduce the air tank pressure.
    - The parking brake knob should pop out when the air pressure falls to the manufacturer's specification (usually between 20 and 40 psi). This causes the spring brakes to come on.
    - Check the rate of air pressure build-up.
    - When the engine is at operating RPM (check the manufacturer's specifications to determine the correct operating RPM), the pressure should build from 85 to 100 psi within 45 seconds in dual air systems.
    - If the vehicle has larger than minimum air tanks, the buildup time can be longer. Check the manufacturer's specifications.
    - In single air systems (built before 1975), pressure typically builds from 50 to 90 psi within 3 minutes with the engine at an idle speed of 600-900 RPM.
    - If air pressure does not build fast enough, your pressure may drop too low during driving. This will require an emergency stop. Don't drive until you get the problem fixed.
  - o Test the air leakage rate.
    - When the air system is fully charged (between 120 and 125 psi), turn off the engine, release the service brake and time the air pressure drop. The loss rate should be less than 2 psi in one minute for single vehicles. It should be less than 3 psi in one minute for combination vehicles.
    - Apply 90 psi or more with the brake pedal. After the initial pressure drop, if air pressure falls more than 3 psi in one minute for single vehicles (4 psi for combination vehicles), the air loss rate is too high.
    - Check for air leaks and fix them before driving or you could lose your brakes while driving.
  - o Check the air compressor governor cut-in and cut-out pressures.
    - Air compressor pumping should start at about 100 psi and stop at about 125 psi. Check the manufacturer's specifications.

- Run the engine at a fast idle. The air governor should cut out the air compressor at the manufacturer's specified pressure. The air pressure shown by your gauge(s) will stop rising.
- With the engine idling, step on and off the brake to reduce the air tank pressure. The compressor should cut in at the manufacturer's specified cut-in pressure. The pressure should begin to rise.
- If the air governor does not work as described above, it may need to be fixed. A governor that does not work right may not keep enough air pressure for safe driving.
  - Test the parking brake. Stop the vehicle, put on the parking brake and gently pull against it in a low gear to test that the parking brake will hold.
  - Test the service brakes.
    - Wait for normal air pressure to build, release the parking brake, move the vehicle forward slowly (about 5 mph) and apply the brakes firmly using the brake pedal.
    - Watch to see if the vehicle pulls to one side, feels unusual or stops slowly.
    - This test can show you problems which you would not know about until you used the brakes on the road.

Using air brakes

Normal stops
Push the brake pedal down. Control the pressure so the vehicle comes to a smooth, safe stop. If you have a manual transmission, don't push the clutch in until the engine rpm is down close to idle. When stopped, select a starting gear.

Braking with antilock brakes
When you brake hard on slippery surfaces in a vehicle without ABS, your wheels may lock up. When your steering wheels lock up, you lose steering control. When your other wheels lock up, you may skid, jackknife, or even spin the vehicle. ABS helps you avoid wheel lock up. The computer senses impending lockup, reduces the braking pressure to a safe level, and you maintain control. You may or may not be able to stop faster with ABS, but you should be able to steer around an obstacle while braking, and avoid skids caused by over braking. Having ABS on only the tractor, only the trailer, or even on only one axle, still gives you more control over the vehicle during braking. Brake normally. When only the tractor has ABS, you should be able to maintain steering control, and there is less chance of jackknifing. But, keep your eye on the trailer and let up on the brakes (if you can safely do so) if it begins to swing out. When only the trailer has ABS, the trailer is less likely to swing out, but if you lose steering control or start a tractor jackknife, let up on the brakes (if you can safely do so) until you gain control. When you drive a tractor-trailer combination with ABS, you should brake as you always have.

In other words:
- Use only the braking force necessary to stop safely and stay in control.
- Brake the same way, regardless of whether you have ABS on the tractor, the trailer, or both.
- As you slow down, monitor your tractor and trailer and back off the brakes (if it is safe to do so) to stay in control.

There is only one exception to this procedure, if you always drive a straight truck or combination with working ABS on all axles, in an emergency stop, you can fully apply the brakes. Without ABS, you still have normal brake functions. Drive and brake as you always have. Remember, if your ABS malfunctions, you still have regular brakes. Drive normally, but get the system serviced soon.

Braking on downgrades

The use of brakes on a long and/or steep downgrade is only a supplement to the braking effect of the engine. Once the vehicle is in the proper low gear, the following is the proper braking technique:
- Apply the brakes just hard enough to feel a definite slowdown.
- When your speed has been reduced to approximately five mph below your "safe" speed, release the brakes. (This application should last for about three seconds.)
- When your speed has increased to your "safe" speed, repeat steps 1 and 2.

For example, if your "safe" speed is 40 mph, you would not apply the brakes until your speed reaches 40 mph. You now apply the brakes hard enough to gradually reduce your speed to 35 mph and then release the brakes. Repeat this as often as necessary until you have reached the end of the downgrade.

Stopping distance

Air brakes increase your stopping distance. Hydraulic brakes (used on cars and light/medium trucks) work instantly. Air brakes take half a second or more for the air to flow through the lines to the brakes. Due to this, vehicles with air brakes require more stopping distance than vehicles with other types of brakes. The total stopping distance for vehicles with air brake systems is made up of four different factors:
- Perception distance - the distance your vehicle travels from the time your eyes see a hazard until your brain recognizes it.
- Reaction distance - the distance your vehicle travels from the time your brain tells your foot to move from the accelerator until the time your foot pushes the brake.
- Brake lag distance - the distance your vehicle travels from the time your foot pushes the air brake until the brake takes hold.
- Braking distance - the distance your vehicle travels between the time the brakes take hold and the vehicle stops.

By adding these distances together, you will get your total stopping distance. The air brake lag distance at 55 mph on dry pavement adds about 32 feet. So at 55 mph for an average driver under good traction and brake conditions, the total stopping distance is over 450 feet.

Brake fading or failure

Brakes are designed so brake shoes or pads rub against the brake drum or disks to slow the vehicle. Braking creates heat, but brakes are designed to take a lot of heat. However, brakes can fade or fail from excessive heat caused by using them too much and not relying on the engine braking effect. Excessive use of the service brakes causes overheating and leads to brake fade. Excessive heat in the brakes causes chemical changes in the lining which reduces friction and causes the brake drums to expand. As the overheated drums expand, the brake shoes and linings have to move farther to contact the drums, and the force of this contact is reduced. Continued overuse may increase brake fade until the vehicle cannot be slowed down or stopped. Brake fade is also affected by adjustment. To safely control a vehicle, every brake must do its share of the work. Brakes out of adjustment will stop doing their share before those that are in adjustment. The other brakes can then overheat and fade, and there will not be enough braking available to control the vehicle(s). Brakes can get out of adjustment quickly, especially when they are hot. Therefore, check brake adjustment often.

Low air pressure

If the low air pressure warning comes on, stop and safely park your vehicle as soon as possible. There might be an air leak in the system. Controlled braking is possible only while enough air remains in the air tanks. The spring brakes will come on when the air pressure drops into the range of 20 to 45 psi. A heavily loaded vehicle will take a long distance to stop because the spring brakes do not work on all axles. Lightly loaded vehicles or vehicles on slippery roads may skid out of control when the spring brakes come on. It is much safer to stop while there is enough air in the tanks to use the foot brakes.

Parking brakes

Any time you park, use the parking brakes, except as noted below. Pull the parking brake control knob out to apply the parking brakes, push it in to release. The control will be a yellow, diamond-shaped knob labeled "parking brakes" on newer vehicles. On older vehicles, it may be a round blue knob or some other shape (including a lever that swings from side to side or up and down). Don't use the parking brakes if the brakes are very hot (from just having come down a steep grade), or if the brakes are very wet in freezing temperatures. If they are used while they are very hot, they can be damaged by the heat. If they are used in freezing temperatures when the brakes are very wet, they can freeze so the vehicle cannot move. Use wheel chocks on a level surface to hold the vehicle. Let hot brakes cool before using the parking brakes. If the brakes are wet, use the brakes lightly while driving in a low gear to heat and dry them. If your vehicle does not have automatic air tank drains, drain your air tanks at the end of each working day to remove moisture and oil. Otherwise, the brakes could fail. Never leave your vehicle unattended without applying the parking brakes or chocking the wheels. The vehicle could roll, causing injury and damage.

Airbrakes Endorsement Tests

Practice Questions

Part One

1. What are the three braking systems?
    a. The parking brake and emergency brake and thermal system
    b. The service brake and parking brake and emergency system.
    c. The service brake and emergency and the inverse system.

2. What is used to make the brakes work?
    a. Compressed Oxygen.
    b. Compressed Nitrogen.
    c. Compressed air.

3. What does the air compressor do?
    a. Pumps air into the air storage tanks.
    b. Keeps the tires inflated to proper pressure
    c. Comes on only if you have to make an emergency stop.

4. What does the air compressor governor control?
    a. It controls emergency warning systems.
    b. It controls when the compressor will pump air into the air storage tanks.
    c. It controls how the compressor will pump air into the air lines.

5. How much compressed air must the storage tanks hold?
    a. At least one hundred and twenty pounds of air.
    b. A maximum of one atmosphere.
    c. Enough air to allow brakes to be used when the air compressor stops working.

6. If oil and water collect in the air tanks what can happen to the brakes?
    a. The brakes can fail.
    b. Brake linings will automatically slip loose
    c. The brakes will work better.

7. No automatic tank drains - when should you drain the air tanks?
    a. Once a week.
    b. Once a month.
    c. Every day.

8. Where will you find the drain valve for each air tank?
    a. In the bottom of the tank.
    b. At the top of the tank.
    c. It is usually found above the tank.

9. What are the two types of air tank drains?
     a. Manually operated. . . Emergency.
     b. Automatic . . . Emergency.
     c. Manually operated. . . Automatic.

10. What is a purpose of an alcohol evaporator?
     a. It takes alcohol from the air system.
     b. It reduces risk of ice in brake valves and other parts in cold weather.
     c. It is designed to save fuel in warm weather.

Part Two

1. How often should you check the alcohol evaporator in cold weather?
     a. Check the alcohol container and fill up as necessary once each week.
     b. Check the alcohol container once each fall before cold weather starts.
     c. Check the alcohol container and fill up as necessary every day.

2. What is a purpose of the safety release valve in the first tank?
     a. It protects the tank and the rest of the system from too much pressure
     b. It protects all of the system from dirt and oil.
     c. It helps build up air pressure quickly without running the engine.

3. What are two other names for the brake pedal?
     a. It can be called the foot valve or the relay valve.
     b. It can be called the foot valve or treadle valve.
     c. It can be called the relay valve or air compressor valve.

4. What can happen if the brake pedal is pressed and released too often?
     a. The brakes will be cooled down as soon as all the hot air is removed.
     b. Air pressure can build up until the brake pressure gauge is broken.
     c. Air can be let out of the system faster than the compressor can replace.

5. Where are foundation brakes found?
     a. At each wheel.
     b. On every other axle.
     c. On the drive wheels only.

6. Where are brake shoes and linings located?
     a. Directly beneath the foot valve.
     b. Inside each brake drum
     c. On the outside of certain brake drums.

7. What happens when a brake lining is pushed against the inside of the drum?
     a. The brakes will always squeal.
     b. This causes friction which slows the vehicle and creates heat.
     c. This causes heat which automatically causes the brakes to lock up.

8. On S-Cam brakes what happens to the air when you push the brake pedal?
   a. Air pressure forces out the push rod and moves the slack adjuster.
   b. Air pressure works only with wedge brakes and not with S-Cam brakes.
   c. Air pressure is converted into hydraulic pressure.

9. Which direction does the S-Cam force brake shoes when brakes are applied?
   a. It presses them against the outside of the brake drum.
   b. It presses them against the inside of the brake drum.
   c. It presses them around the brake drum.

10. If the air compressor begins to leak what keeps air in the tanks?
    a. The slack adjusters.
    b. The alcohol evaporator.
    c. The one-way check valve.

Part Three

1. What is one kind of gauge that is required for vehicles with air brakes?
   a. An air temperature gauge.
   b. An air pressure gauge
   c. An oil pressure gauge.

2. What kind of warning signal is required on vehicles with air brakes?
   a. A high air pressure warning signal.
   b. A low air pressure warning signal.
   c. A changing air pressure warning signal.

3. What are the three types of low air pressure warning devices?
   a. A siren . . . or a horn . . . or 4-way flashers.
   b. A red light . . . or a buzzer . . . or a wigwag.
   c. An air horn . . . or an amber light . . . or a whistle.

4. What is used to turn on the stop lights in an air brakes system?
   a. An electric switch that works by air pressure
   b. A computer.
   c. A motion sensor in the wheels.

5. In normal driving parking and emergency brakes are usually held back by?
   a. Electric relay switches.
   b. Wheel chocks.
   c. Air pressure.

6. The effectiveness of the spring brakes depends on the adjustment of?
   a. Emergency brakes.
   b. Service brakes.
   c. Front wheel brakes.

7. Why do some buses have a separate air tank to release spring brakes?
    a. So you can move the vehicle in an emergency.
    b. To simplify servicing the air brake system.
    c. So that the brakes will release quicker.

8. What is a dual air brake system?
    a. Two separate air brake systems with a single set of brake controls.
    b. One air brake system with two sets of brake controls.
    c. Two separate air brake systems with two sets of brake controls.

9. What should you look for in checking an air compressor belt?
    a. Check for belts that are the wrong color.
    b. Check for belts that are not made of rubber.
    c. Check belts for excessive wear and cracks and tightness.

10. What should you do before checking free play in manual slack adjusters?
    a. Park in a secure location and remove all wheel chocks.
    b. Park on level ground so that the wheels will not have to be chocked.
    c. Park on level ground and chock the wheels and release parking brakes.

Part Four

1. Combination vehicle: brakes released. The maximum air released?
    a. One pound per square inch.
    b. Less than two pounds per square inch
    c. Less than three pounds per square inch.

2. Single vehicle: brakes released. Maximum air leakage in one minute?
    a. One pound per square inch.
    b. Less than two pounds per square inch.
    c. Less than three pounds per square inch.

3. After applying brakes fully, maximum air loss in one minute - single vehicles?
    a. Two pounds per square inch.
    b. Three pounds per square inch.
    c. Four pounds per square inch.

4. After applying brakes fully max. air loss in one minute - combination vehicles?
    a. Two pounds per square inch.
    b. Three pounds per square inch.
    c. Four pounds per square inch.

5. When should the air governor cut out the air compressor?
    a. At about the manufacturer specified air pressure.
    b. At about ten pounds per square inch.
    c. At about one hundred and ten pounds per square inch.

6. When making a normal stop when should you push in the clutch?
   a. Experienced drivers do not use the clutch.
   b. Do not push in the clutch until there is vibration.
   c. Do not push the clutch in until the engine R.P.M.'s are down close to idle.

7. When making a very quick stop you should brake so that you?
   a. Can turn quickly to get out the way of hazards.
   b. Skid to maximize stopping distance.
   c. Stay in a straight line and can steer.

8. What is another name for controlled braking?
   a. Steady braking.
   b. Hard braking.
   c. Squeeze braking.

9. What is stab braking?
   a. Putting the brakes on hard without locking the wheels or turning
   b. Pressing the brake pedal hard and releasing brakes when wheels lock up.
   c. Applying a constant pressure to the brakes.

10. Why does air braking take more time than hydraulic braking?
    a. Because air brakes are generally used on longer vehicles
    b. Because it takes time for air to flow through the lines to the brakes.
    c. Because air moves through the lines much slower than oil does.

Answer Key

Part One

1. B: The service brake and parking brake and emergency system.

2. C: Compressed air.

3. A: Pumps air into the air storage tanks.

4. B: It controls when the compressor will pump air into the air storage tanks.

5. C: Enough air to allow brakes to be used when the air compressor stops working.

6. A: The brakes can fail.

7. C: Every day.

8. A: In the bottom of the tank.

9. C: Manually operated. . . Automatic.

10. B: It reduces risk of ice in brake valves and other parts in cold weather.

Part Two

1. C: Check the alcohol container and fill up as necessary every day.

2. A: It protects the tank and the rest of the system from too much pressure

3. B: It can be called the foot valve or treadle valve.

4. C: Air can be let out of the system faster than the compressor can replace.

5. A: At each wheel.

6. B: Inside each brake drum

7. B: This causes friction which slows the vehicle and creates heat.

8. A: Air pressure forces out the push rod and moves the slack adjuster.

9. B: It presses them against the inside of the brake drum.

10. C: The one-way check valve.

Part Three

1. B: An air pressure gauge

2. B: A low air pressure warning signal.

3. B: A red light . . . or a buzzer . . . or a wigwag.

4. A: An electric switch that works by air pressure

5. C: Air pressure.

6. B: Service brakes.

7. A: So you can move the vehicle in an emergency.

8. A: Two separate air brake systems with a single set of brake controls.

9. C: Check belts for excessive wear and cracks and tightness.

10. C: Park on level ground and chock the wheels and release parking brakes.

Part Four

1. C: Less than three pounds per square inch.

2. B: Less than two pounds per square inch.

3. B: Three pounds per square inch.

4. C: Four pounds per square inch.

5. A: At about the manufacturer specified air pressure.

6. C: Do not push the clutch in until the engine R.P.M.'s are down close to idle.

7. C: Stay in a straight line and can steer.

8. C: Squeeze braking.

9. B: Pressing the brake pedal hard and releasing brakes when wheels lock up.

10. B: Because it takes time for air to flow through the lines to the brakes.

Secret Key #1 - Time is Your Greatest Enemy

Pace Yourself

Wear a watch. At the beginning of the test, check the time (or start a chronometer on your watch to count the minutes), and check the time after every few questions to make sure you are "on schedule."

If you are forced to speed up, do it efficiently. Usually one or more answer choices can be eliminated without too much difficulty. Above all, don't panic. Don't speed up and just begin guessing at random choices. By pacing yourself, and continually monitoring your progress against your watch, you will always know exactly how far ahead or behind you are with your available time. If you find that you are one minute behind on the test, don't skip one question without spending any time on it, just to catch back up. Take 15 fewer seconds on the next four questions, and after four questions you'll have caught back up. Once you catch back up, you can continue working each problem at your normal pace.

Furthermore, don't dwell on the problems that you were rushed on. If a problem was taking up too much time and you made a hurried guess, it must be difficult. The difficult questions are the ones you are most likely to miss anyway, so it isn't a big loss. It is better to end with more time than you need than to run out of time.

Lastly, sometimes it is beneficial to slow down if you are constantly getting ahead of time. You are always more likely to catch a careless mistake by working more slowly than quickly, and among very high-scoring test takers (those who are likely to have lots of time left over), careless errors affect the score more than mastery of material.

Secret Key #2 - Guessing is not Guesswork

You probably know that guessing is a good idea. Unlike other standardized tests, there is no penalty for getting a wrong answer. Even if you have no idea about a question, you still have a 20-25% chance of getting it right.

Most test takers do not understand the impact that proper guessing can have on their score. Unless you score extremely high, guessing will significantly contribute to your final score.

Monkeys Take the Test

What most test takers don't realize is that to insure that 20-25% chance, you have to guess randomly. If you put 20 monkeys in a room to take this test, assuming they answered once per question and behaved themselves, on average they would get 20-25% of the questions correct. Put 20 test takers in the room, and the average will be much lower among guessed questions. Why?
1. The test writers intentionally write deceptive answer choices that "look" right. A test taker has no idea about a question, so he picks the "best looking" answer, which is often wrong. The monkey has no idea what looks good and what doesn't, so it will consistently be right about 20-25% of the time.
2. Test takers will eliminate answer choices from the guessing pool based on a hunch or intuition. Simple but correct answers often get excluded, leaving a 0% chance of being correct. The monkey has no clue, and often gets lucky with the best choice.

This is why the process of elimination endorsed by most test courses is flawed and detrimental to your performance. Test takers don't guess; they make an ignorant stab in the dark that is usually worse than random.

$5 Challenge

Let me introduce one of the most valuable ideas of this course—the $5 challenge:

You only mark your "best guess" if you are willing to bet $5 on it.
You only eliminate choices from guessing if you are willing to bet $5 on it.

Why $5? Five dollars is an amount of money that is small yet not insignificant, and can really add up fast (20 questions could cost you $100). Likewise, each answer choice on one question of the test will have a small impact on your overall score, but it can really add up to a lot of points in the end.

The process of elimination IS valuable. The following shows your chance of guessing it right:

If you eliminate wrong answer choices until only this many remain:	Chance of getting it correct:
1	100%
2	50%
3	33%

However, if you accidentally eliminate the right answer or go on a hunch for an incorrect answer, your chances drop dramatically—to 0%. By guessing among all the answer choices, you are GUARANTEED to have a shot at the right answer.

That's why the $5 test is so valuable. If you give up the advantage and safety of a pure guess, it had better be worth the risk.

What we still haven't covered is how to be sure that whatever guess you make is truly random. Here's the easiest way:

Always pick the first answer choice among those remaining.

Such a technique means that you have decided, **before you see a single test question**, exactly how you are going to guess, and since the order of choices tells you nothing about which one is correct, this guessing technique is perfectly random.

This section is not meant to scare you away from making educated guesses or eliminating choices; you just need to define when a choice is worth eliminating. The $5 test, along with a pre-defined random guessing strategy, is the best way to make sure you reap all of the benefits of guessing.

Secret Key #3 - Practice Smarter, Not Harder

Many test takers delay the test preparation process because they dread the awful amounts of practice time they think necessary to succeed on the test. We have refined an effective method that will take you only a fraction of the time.

There are a number of "obstacles" in the path to success. Among these are answering questions, finishing in time, and mastering test-taking strategies. All must be executed on the day of the test at peak performance, or your score will suffer. The test is a mental marathon that has a large impact on your future.

Just like a marathon runner, it is important to work your way up to the full challenge. So first you just worry about questions, and then time, and finally strategy:

Success Strategy

1. Find a good source for practice tests.
2. If you are willing to make a larger time investment, consider using more than one study guide. Often the different approaches of multiple authors will help you "get" difficult concepts.
3. Take a practice test with no time constraints, with all study helps, "open book." Take your time with questions and focus on applying strategies.
4. Take a practice test with time constraints, with all guides, "open book."
5. Take a final practice test without open material and with time limits.

If you have time to take more practice tests, just repeat step 5. By gradually exposing yourself to the full rigors of the test environment, you will condition your mind to the stress of test day and maximize your success.

Secret Key #4 - Prepare, Don't Procrastinate

Let me state an obvious fact: if you take the test three times, you will probably get three different scores. This is due to the way you feel on test day, the level of preparedness you have, and the version of the test you see. Despite the test writers' claims to the contrary, some versions of the test WILL be easier for you than others.

Since your future depends so much on your score, you should maximize your chances of success. In order to maximize the likelihood of success, you've got to prepare in advance. This means taking practice tests and spending time learning the information and test taking strategies you will need to succeed.

Never go take the actual test as a "practice" test, expecting that you can just take it again if you need to. Take all the practice tests you can on your own, but when you go to take the official test, be prepared, be focused, and do your best the first time!

Secret Key #5 - Test Yourself

Everyone knows that time is money. There is no need to spend too much of your time or too little of your time preparing for the test. You should only spend as much of your precious time preparing as is necessary for you to get the score you need.

Once you have taken a practice test under real conditions of time constraints, then you will know if you are ready for the test or not.

If you have scored extremely high the first time that you take the practice test, then there is not much point in spending countless hours studying. You are already there.

Benchmark your abilities by retaking practice tests and seeing how much you have improved. Once you consistently score high enough to guarantee success, then you are ready.

If you have scored well below where you need, then knuckle down and begin studying in earnest. Check your improvement regularly through the use of practice tests under real conditions. Above all, don't worry, panic, or give up. The key is perseverance!

Then, when you go to take the test, remain confident and remember how well you did on the practice tests. If you can score high enough on a practice test, then you can do the same on the real thing.

General Strategies

The most important thing you can do is to ignore your fears and jump into the test immediately. Do not be overwhelmed by any strange-sounding terms. You have to jump into the test like jumping into a pool—all at once is the easiest way.

Make Predictions

As you read and understand the question, try to guess what the answer will be. Remember that several of the answer choices are wrong, and once you begin reading them, your mind will immediately become cluttered with answer choices designed to throw you off. Your mind is typically the most focused immediately after you have read the question and digested its contents. If you can, try to predict what the correct answer will be. You may be surprised at what you can predict.

Quickly scan the choices and see if your prediction is in the listed answer choices. If it is, then you can be quite confident that you have the right answer. It still won't hurt to check the other answer choices, but most of the time, you've got it!

Answer the Question

It may seem obvious to only pick answer choices that answer the question, but the test writers can create some excellent answer choices that are wrong. Don't pick an answer just because it sounds right, or you believe it to be true. It MUST answer the question. Once you've made your selection, always go back and check it against the question and make sure that you didn't misread the question and that the answer choice does answer the question posed.

Benchmark

After you read the first answer choice, decide if you think it sounds correct or not. If it doesn't, move on to the next answer choice. If it does, mentally mark that answer choice. This doesn't mean that you've definitely selected it as your answer choice, it just means that it's the best you've seen thus far. Go ahead and read the next choice. If the next choice is worse than the one you've already selected, keep going to the next answer choice. If the next choice is better than the choice you've already selected, mentally mark the new answer choice as your best guess.

The first answer choice that you select becomes your standard. Every other answer choice must be benchmarked against that standard. That choice is correct until proven otherwise by another answer choice beating it out. Once you've decided that no other answer choice seems as good, do one final check to ensure that your answer choice answers the question posed.

Valid Information

Don't discount any of the information provided in the question. Every piece of information may be necessary to determine the correct answer. None of the information in the question is there to throw you off (while the answer choices will certainly have information to throw you off). If two seemingly unrelated topics are discussed, don't ignore either. You can be confident there is a relationship, or it wouldn't be included in the question, and you are probably going to have to determine what is that relationship to find the answer.

Avoid "Fact Traps"

Don't get distracted by a choice that is factually true. Your search is for the answer that answers the question. Stay focused and don't fall for an answer that is true but irrelevant. Always go back to the question and make sure you're choosing an answer that actually answers the question and is not just a true statement. An answer can be factually correct, but it MUST answer the question asked. Additionally, two answers can both be seemingly correct, so be sure to read all of the answer choices, and make sure that you get the one that BEST answers the question.

Milk the Question

Some of the questions may throw you completely off. They might deal with a subject you have not been exposed to, or one that you haven't reviewed in years. While your lack of knowledge about the subject will be a hindrance, the question itself can give you many clues that will help you find the correct answer. Read the question carefully and look for clues. Watch particularly for adjectives and nouns describing difficult terms or words that you don't recognize. Regardless of whether you completely understand a word or not, replacing it with a synonym, either provided or one you more familiar with, may help you to understand what the questions are asking. Rather than wracking your mind about specific detailed information concerning a difficult term or word, try to use mental substitutes that are easier to understand.

The Trap of Familiarity

Don't just choose a word because you recognize it. On difficult questions, you may not recognize a number of words in the answer choices. The test writers don't put "make-believe" words on the test, so don't think that just because you only recognize all the words in one answer choice that that answer choice must be correct. If you only recognize words in one answer choice, then focus on that one. Is it correct? Try your best to determine if it is correct. If it is, that's great. If not, eliminate it. Each word and answer choice you eliminate increases your chances of getting the question correct, even if you then have to guess among the unfamiliar choices.

Eliminate Answers

Eliminate choices as soon as you realize they are wrong. But be careful! Make sure you consider all of the possible answer choices. Just because one appears right, doesn't mean that the next one won't be even better! The test writers will usually put more than one good answer choice for every question, so read all of them. Don't worry if you are stuck between two that seem right. By getting down to just two remaining possible choices, your odds are now 50/50. Rather than wasting too much time, play the odds. You are guessing, but guessing wisely because you've been able to knock out some of the answer choices that you know are wrong. If you are eliminating choices and realize that the last answer choice you are left with is also obviously wrong, don't panic. Start over and consider each choice again. There may easily be something that you missed the first time and will realize on the second pass.

Tough Questions

If you are stumped on a problem or it appears too hard or too difficult, don't waste time. Move on! Remember though, if you can quickly check for obviously incorrect answer choices, your chances of guessing correctly are greatly improved. Before you completely give up, at least try to knock out a couple of possible answers. Eliminate what you can and then guess at the remaining answer choices before moving on.

Brainstorm

If you get stuck on a difficult question, spend a few seconds quickly brainstorming. Run through the complete list of possible answer choices. Look at each choice and ask yourself, "Could this answer the question satisfactorily?" Go through each answer choice and consider it independently of the others. By systematically going through all possibilities, you may find something that you would otherwise overlook. Remember though that when you get stuck, it's important to try to keep moving.

Read Carefully

Understand the problem. Read the question and answer choices carefully. Don't miss the question because you misread the terms. You have plenty of time to read each question thoroughly and make sure you understand what is being asked. Yet a happy medium must be attained, so don't waste too much time. You must read carefully, but efficiently.

Face Value

When in doubt, use common sense. Always accept the situation in the problem at face value. Don't read too much into it. These problems will not require you to make huge leaps of logic. The test writers aren't trying to throw you off with a cheap trick. If you have to go beyond creativity and make a leap of logic in order to have an answer choice answer the question, then you should look at the other answer choices. Don't overcomplicate the problem by creating theoretical relationships or explanations that will warp time or space. These are normal problems rooted in reality. It's just that the applicable relationship or explanation may not be readily apparent and you have to figure things out. Use your common sense to interpret anything that isn't clear.

Prefixes

If you're having trouble with a word in the question or answer choices, try dissecting it. Take advantage of every clue that the word might include. Prefixes and suffixes can be a huge help. Usually they allow you to determine a basic meaning. Pre- means before, post- means after, pro - is positive, de- is negative. From these prefixes and suffixes, you can get an idea of the general meaning of the word and try to put it into context. Beware though of any traps. Just because con- is the opposite of pro-, doesn't necessarily mean congress is the opposite of progress!

Hedge Phrases

Watch out for critical hedge phrases, led off with words such as "likely," "may," "can," "sometimes," "often," "almost," "mostly," "usually," "generally," "rarely," and "sometimes." Question writers insert these hedge phrases to cover every possibility. Often an answer choice will be wrong simply because it leaves no room for exception. Unless the situation calls for them, avoid answer choices that have definitive words like "exactly," and "always."

Switchback Words

Stay alert for "switchbacks." These are the words and phrases frequently used to alert you to shifts in thought. The most common switchback word is "but." Others include "although," "however," "nevertheless," "on the other hand," "even though," "while," "in spite of," "despite," and "regardless of."

New Information

Correct answer choices will rarely have completely new information included. Answer choices typically are straightforward reflections of the material asked about and will directly relate to the question. If a new piece of information is included in an answer choice that doesn't even seem to relate to the topic being asked about, then that answer choice is likely incorrect. All of the information needed to answer the question is usually provided for you in the question. You should not have to make guesses that are unsupported or choose answer choices that require unknown information that cannot be reasoned from what is given.

Time Management

On technical questions, don't get lost on the technical terms. Don't spend too much time on any one question. If you don't know what a term means, then odds are you aren't going to get much further since you don't have a dictionary. You should be able to immediately recognize whether or not you know a term. If you don't, work with the other clues that you have—the other answer choices and terms provided—but don't waste too much time trying to figure out a difficult term that you don't know.

Contextual Clues

Look for contextual clues. An answer can be right but not the correct answer. The contextual clues will help you find the answer that is most right and is correct. Understand the context in which a phrase or statement is made. This will help you make important distinctions.

Don't Panic

Panicking will not answer any questions for you; therefore, it isn't helpful. When you first see the question, if your mind goes blank, take a deep breath. Force yourself to mechanically go through the steps of solving the problem using the strategies you've learned.

Pace Yourself

Don't get clock fever. It's easy to be overwhelmed when you're looking at a page full of questions, your mind is full of random thoughts and feeling confused, and the clock is ticking down faster than you would like. Calm down and maintain the pace that you have set for yourself. As long as you are on track by monitoring your pace, you are guaranteed to have enough time for yourself. When you get to the last few minutes of the test, it may seem like you won't have enough time left, but if you only have as many questions as you should have left at that point, then you're right on track!

Answer Selection

The best way to pick an answer choice is to eliminate all of those that are wrong, until only one is left and confirm that is the correct answer. Sometimes though, an answer choice may immediately look right. Be careful! Take a second to make sure that the other choices are not equally obvious. Don't make a hasty mistake. There are only two times that you should stop before checking other answers. First is when you are positive that the answer choice you have selected is correct. Second is when time is almost out and you have to make a quick guess!

Check Your Work

Since you will probably not know every term listed and the answer to every question, it is important that you get credit for the ones that you do know. Don't miss any questions through careless mistakes. If at all possible, try to take a second to look back over your answer selection and make sure you've selected the correct answer choice and haven't made a costly careless mistake (such as marking an answer choice that you didn't mean to mark). The time it takes for this quick double check should more than pay for itself in caught mistakes.

Beware of Directly Quoted Answers

Sometimes an answer choice will repeat word for word a portion of the question or reference section. However, beware of such exact duplication. It may be a trap! More than likely, the correct choice will paraphrase or summarize a point, rather than being exactly the same wording.

Slang

Scientific sounding answers are better than slang ones. An answer choice that begins "To compare the outcomes…" is much more likely to be correct than one that begins "Because some people insisted…"

Extreme Statements

Avoid wild answers that throw out highly controversial ideas that are proclaimed as established fact. An answer choice that states the "process should used in certain situations, if…" is much more likely to be correct than one that states the "process should be discontinued completely." The first is a calm rational statement and doesn't even make a definitive, uncompromising stance, using a hedge word "if" to provide wiggle room, whereas the second choice is a radical idea and far more extreme.

Answer Choice Families

When you have two or more answer choices that are direct opposites or parallels, one of them is usually the correct answer. For instance, if one answer choice states "x increases" and another answer choice states "x decreases" or "y increases," then those two or three answer choices are very similar in construction and fall into the same family of answer choices. A family of answer choices consists of two or three answer choices, very similar in construction, but often with directly opposite meanings. Usually the correct answer choice will be in that family of answer choices. The "odd man out" or answer choice that doesn't seem to fit the parallel construction of the other answer choices is more likely to be incorrect.

Special Report: How to Overcome Test Anxiety

The very nature of tests caters to some level of anxiety, nervousness, or tension, just as we feel for any important event that occurs in our lives. A little bit of anxiety or nervousness can be a good thing. It helps us with motivation, and makes achievement just that much sweeter. However, too much anxiety can be a problem, especially if it hinders our ability to function and perform.

"Test anxiety," is the term that refers to the emotional reactions that some test-takers experience when faced with a test or exam. Having a fear of testing and exams is based upon a rational fear, since the test-taker's performance can shape the course of an academic career. Nevertheless, experiencing excessive fear of examinations will only interfere with the test-taker's ability to perform and chance to be successful.

There are a large variety of causes that can contribute to the development and sensation of test anxiety. These include, but are not limited to, lack of preparation and worrying about issues surrounding the test.

Lack of Preparation

Lack of preparation can be identified by the following behaviors or situations:

Not scheduling enough time to study, and therefore cramming the night before the test or exam
Managing time poorly, to create the sensation that there is not enough time to do everything
Failing to organize the text information in advance, so that the study material consists of the entire text and not simply the pertinent information
Poor overall studying habits

Worrying, on the other hand, can be related to both the test taker, or many other factors around him/her that will be affected by the results of the test. These include worrying about:

Previous performances on similar exams, or exams in general
How friends and other students are achieving
The negative consequences that will result from a poor grade or failure

There are three primary elements to test anxiety. Physical components, which involve the same typical bodily reactions as those to acute anxiety (to be discussed below). Emotional factors have to do with fear or panic. Mental or cognitive issues concerning attention spans and memory abilities.

Physical Signals

There are many different symptoms of test anxiety, and these are not limited to mental and emotional strain. Frequently there are a range of physical signals that will let a test taker know that he/she is suffering from test anxiety. These bodily changes can include the following:

Perspiring
Sweaty palms
Wet, trembling hands
Nausea
Dry mouth
A knot in the stomach
Headache
Faintness
Muscle tension
Aching shoulders, back and neck
Rapid heart beat
Feeling too hot/cold

To recognize the sensation of test anxiety, a test-taker should monitor him/herself for the following sensations:

The physical distress symptoms as listed above
Emotional sensitivity, expressing emotional feelings such as the need to cry or laugh too much, or a sensation of anger or helplessness
A decreased ability to think, causing the test-taker to blank out or have racing thoughts that are hard to organize or control.

Though most students will feel some level of anxiety when faced with a test or exam, the majority can cope with that anxiety and maintain it at a manageable level. However, those who cannot are faced with a very real and very serious condition, which can and should be controlled for the immeasurable benefit of this sufferer.

Naturally, these sensations lead to negative results for the testing experience. The most common effects of test anxiety have to do with nervousness and mental blocking.

Nervousness

Nervousness can appear in several different levels:

The test-taker's difficulty, or even inability to read and understand the questions on the test
The difficulty or inability to organize thoughts to a coherent form
The difficulty or inability to recall key words and concepts relating to the testing questions (especially essays)
The receipt of poor grades on a test, though the test material was well known by the test taker

Conversely, a person may also experience mental blocking, which involves:

Blanking out on test questions
Only remembering the correct answers to the questions when the test has already finished.

Fortunately for test anxiety sufferers, beating these feelings, to a large degree, has to do with proper preparation. When a test taker has a feeling of preparedness, then anxiety will be dramatically lessened.

The first step to resolving anxiety issues is to distinguish which of the two types of anxiety are being suffered. If the anxiety is a direct result of a lack of preparation, this should be considered a normal reaction, and the anxiety level (as opposed to the test results) shouldn't be anything to worry about. However, if, when adequately prepared, the test-taker still panics, blanks out, or seems to overreact, this is not a fully rational reaction. While this can be considered normal too, there are many ways to combat and overcome these effects.

Remember that anxiety cannot be entirely eliminated, however, there are ways to minimize it, to make the anxiety easier to manage. Preparation is one of the best ways to minimize test anxiety. Therefore the following techniques are wise in order to best fight off any anxiety that may want to build.

To begin with, try to avoid cramming before a test, whenever it is possible. By trying to memorize an entire term's worth of information in one day, you'll be shocking your system, and not giving yourself a very good chance to absorb the information. This is an easy path to anxiety, so for those who suffer from test anxiety, cramming should not even be considered an option.

Instead of cramming, work throughout the semester to combine all of the material which is presented throughout the semester, and work on it gradually as the course goes by, making sure to master the main concepts first, leaving minor details for a week or so before the test.

To study for the upcoming exam, be sure to pose questions that may be on the examination, to gauge the ability to answer them by integrating the ideas from your texts, notes and lectures, as well as any supplementary readings.

If it is truly impossible to cover all of the information that was covered in that particular term, concentrate on the most important portions, that can be covered very well. Learn these concepts as best as possible, so that when the test comes, a goal can be made to use these concepts as presentations of your knowledge.

In addition to study habits, changes in attitude are critical to beating a struggle with test anxiety. In fact, an improvement of the perspective over the entire test-taking experience can actually help a test taker to enjoy studying and therefore improve the overall experience. Be certain not to overemphasize the significance of the grade - know that the result of the test is neither a reflection of self worth, nor is it a measure of intelligence; one grade will not predict a person's future success.

To improve an overall testing outlook, the following steps should be tried:

Keeping in mind that the most reasonable expectation for taking a test is to expect to try to demonstrate as much of what you know as you possibly can.

Reminding ourselves that a test is only one test; this is not the only one, and there will be others.

The thought of thinking of oneself in an irrational, all-or-nothing term should be avoided at all costs.

A reward should be designated for after the test, so there's something to look forward to. Whether it be going to a movie, going out to eat, or simply visiting friends, schedule it in advance, and do it no matter what result is expected on the exam.

Test-takers should also keep in mind that the basics are some of the most important things, even beyond anti-anxiety techniques and studying. Never neglect the basic social, emotional and biological needs, in order to try to absorb information. In order to best achieve, these three factors must be held as just as important as the studying itself.

Study Steps

Remember the following important steps for studying:

Maintain healthy nutrition and exercise habits. Continue both your recreational activities and social pass times. These both contribute to your physical and emotional well being.

Be certain to get a good amount of sleep, especially the night before the test, because when you're overtired you are not able to perform to the best of your best ability.

Keep the studying pace to a moderate level by taking breaks when they are needed, and varying the work whenever possible, to keep the mind fresh instead of getting bored.

When enough studying has been done that all the material that can be learned has been learned, and the test taker is prepared for the test, stop studying and do something relaxing such as listening to music, watching a movie, or taking a warm bubble bath.

There are also many other techniques to minimize the uneasiness or apprehension that is experienced along with test anxiety before, during, or even after the examination. In fact, there are a great deal of things that can be done to stop anxiety from interfering with lifestyle and performance. Again, remember that anxiety will not be eliminated entirely, and it shouldn't be. Otherwise that "up" feeling for exams would not exist, and most of us depend on that sensation to perform better than usual. However, this anxiety has to be at a level that is manageable.

Of course, as we have just discussed, being prepared for the exam is half the battle right away. Attending all classes, finding out what knowledge will be expected on the exam, and knowing the exam schedules are easy steps to lowering anxiety. Keeping up with work will remove the need to cram, and efficient study habits will eliminate wasted time. Studying should be done in an ideal location for concentration, so that it is simple to become interested in the material and give it complete attention. A method such as SQ3R (Survey, Question, Read, Recite, Review) is a wonderful key to follow to make sure that the study habits are as effective as possible, especially in the case of learning from a textbook. Flashcards are great techniques for memorization. Learning to take good notes will mean that notes will be full of useful information, so that less sifting will need to be done to seek out what is pertinent for studying. Reviewing notes after class and then again on occasion will keep the information fresh in the mind. From notes that have been taken summary sheets and outlines can be made for simpler reviewing.

A study group can also be a very motivational and helpful place to study, as there will be a sharing of ideas, all of the minds can work together, to make sure that everyone understands, and the studying will be made more interesting because it will be a social occasion.

Basically, though, as long as the test-taker remains organized and self confident, with efficient study habits, less time will need to be spent studying, and higher grades will be achieved.

To become self confident, there are many useful steps. The first of these is "self talk." It has been shown through extensive research, that self-talk for students who suffer from test anxiety, should be well monitored, in order to make sure that it contributes to self confidence as opposed to sinking the student. Frequently the self talk of test-anxious students is negative or self-defeating, thinking that everyone else is smarter and faster, that they always mess up, and that if they don't do well, they'll fail the entire course. It is important to decreasing anxiety that awareness is made of self talk. Try writing any negative self thoughts and then disputing them with a positive statement instead. Begin self-encouragement as though it was a friend speaking. Repeat positive statements to help reprogram the mind to believing in successes instead of failures.

Helpful Techniques

Other extremely helpful techniques include:

Self-visualization of doing well and reaching goals
While aiming for an "A" level of understanding, don't try to "overprotect" by setting your expectations lower. This will only convince the mind to stop studying in order to meet the lower expectations.
Don't make comparisons with the results or habits of other students. These are individual factors, and different things work for different people, causing different results.
Strive to become an expert in learning what works well, and what can be done in order to improve. Consider collecting this data in a journal.
Create rewards for after studying instead of doing things before studying that will only turn into avoidance behaviors.
Make a practice of relaxing - by using methods such as progressive relaxation, self-hypnosis, guided imagery, etc - in order to make relaxation an automatic sensation.
Work on creating a state of relaxed concentration so that concentrating will take on the focus of the mind, so that none will be wasted on worrying.
Take good care of the physical self by eating well and getting enough sleep.
Plan in time for exercise and stick to this plan.

Beyond these techniques, there are other methods to be used before, during and after the test that will help the test-taker perform well in addition to overcoming anxiety.

Before the exam comes the academic preparation. This involves establishing a study schedule and beginning at least one week before the actual date of the test. By doing this, the anxiety of not having enough time to study for the test will be automatically eliminated. Moreover, this will make the studying a much more effective experience, ensuring that the learning will be an easier process. This relieves much undue pressure on the test-taker.

Summary sheets, note cards, and flash cards with the main concepts and examples of these main concepts should be prepared in advance of the actual studying time. A topic should never be eliminated from this process. By omitting a topic because it isn't expected to be on the test is only setting up the test-taker for anxiety should it actually appear on the exam. Utilize the course syllabus for laying out the topics that should be studied. Carefully go over the notes that were made in class, paying special attention to any of the issues that the professor took special care to emphasize while lecturing in class. In the textbooks, use the chapter review, or if possible, the chapter tests, to begin your review.

It may even be possible to ask the instructor what information will be covered on the exam, or what the format of the exam will be (for example, multiple choice, essay, free form, true-false). Additionally, see if it is possible to find out how many questions will be on the test. If a review sheet or sample test has been offered by the professor, make good use of it, above anything else, for the preparation for the test. Another great resource for getting to know the examination is reviewing tests from previous semesters. Use these tests to review, and aim to achieve a 100% score on each of the possible topics. With a few exceptions, the goal that you set for yourself is the highest one that you will reach.

Take all of the questions that were assigned as homework, and rework them to any other possible course material. The more problems reworked, the more skill and confidence will form as a result. When forming the solution to a problem, write out each of the steps. Don't simply do head work. By doing as many steps on paper as possible, much clarification and therefore confidence will be formed. Do this with as many homework problems as possible, before checking the answers. By checking the answer after each problem, a reinforcement will exist, that will not be on the exam. Study situations should be as exam-like as possible, to prime the test-taker's system for the experience. By waiting to check the answers at the end, a psychological advantage will be formed, to decrease the stress factor.

Another fantastic reason for not cramming is the avoidance of confusion in concepts, especially when it comes to mathematics. 8-10 hours of study will become one hundred percent more effective if it is spread out over a week or at least several days, instead of doing it all in one sitting. Recognize that the human brain requires time in order to assimilate new material, so frequent breaks and a span of study time over several days will be much more beneficial.

Additionally, don't study right up until the point of the exam. Studying should stop a minimum of one hour before the exam begins. This allows the brain to rest and put things in their proper order. This will also provide the time to become as relaxed as possible when going into the examination room. The test-taker will also have time to eat well and eat sensibly. Know that the brain needs food as much as the rest of the body. With enough food and enough sleep, as well as a relaxed attitude, the body and the mind are primed for success.

Avoid any anxious classmates who are talking about the exam. These students only spread anxiety, and are not worth sharing the anxious sentimentalities.

Before the test also involves creating a positive attitude, so mental preparation should also be a point of concentration. There are many keys to creating a positive attitude. Should fears become rushing in, make a visualization of taking the exam, doing well, and seeing an A written on the paper. Write out a list of affirmations that will bring a feeling of confidence, such as "I am doing well in my English class," "I studied well and know my material," "I enjoy this class." Even if the affirmations aren't believed at first, it sends a positive message to the subconscious which will result in an alteration of the overall belief system, which is the system that creates reality.

If a sensation of panic begins, work with the fear and imagine the very worst! Work through the entire scenario of not passing the test, failing the entire course, and dropping out of school, followed by not getting a job, and pushing a shopping cart through the dark alley where you'll live. This will place things into perspective! Then, practice deep breathing and create a visualization of the opposite situation - achieving an "A" on the exam, passing the entire course, receiving the degree at a graduation ceremony.

On the day of the test, there are many things to be done to ensure the best results, as well as the most calm outlook. The following stages are suggested in order to maximize test-taking potential:

Begin the examination day with a moderate breakfast, and avoid any coffee or beverages with caffeine if the test taker is prone to jitters. Even people who are used to managing caffeine can feel jittery or light-headed when it is taken on a test day.
Attempt to do something that is relaxing before the examination begins. As last minute cramming clouds the mastering of overall concepts, it is better to use this time to create a calming outlook.
Be certain to arrive at the test location well in advance, in order to provide time to select a location that is away from doors, windows and other distractions, as well as giving enough time to relax before the test begins.
Keep away from anxiety generating classmates who will upset the sensation of stability and relaxation that is being attempted before the exam.
Should the waiting period before the exam begins cause anxiety, create a self-distraction by reading a light magazine or something else that is relaxing and simple.

During the exam itself, read the entire exam from beginning to end, and find out how much time should be allotted to each individual problem. Once writing the exam, should more time be taken for a problem, it should be abandoned, in order to begin another problem. If there is time at the end, the unfinished problem can always be returned to and completed.

Read the instructions very carefully - twice - so that unpleasant surprises won't follow during or after the exam has ended.

When writing the exam, pretend that the situation is actually simply the completion of homework within a library, or at home. This will assist in forming a relaxed atmosphere, and will allow the brain extra focus for the complex thinking function.

Begin the exam with all of the questions with which the most confidence is felt. This will build the confidence level regarding the entire exam and will begin a quality momentum. This will also create encouragement for trying the problems where uncertainty resides.

Going with the "gut instinct" is always the way to go when solving a problem. Second guessing should be avoided at all costs. Have confidence in the ability to do well.

For essay questions, create an outline in advance that will keep the mind organized and make certain that all of the points are remembered. For multiple choice, read every answer, even if the correct one has been spotted - a better one may exist.

Continue at a pace that is reasonable and not rushed, in order to be able to work carefully. Provide enough time to go over the answers at the end, to check for small errors that can be corrected.

Should a feeling of panic begin, breathe deeply, and think of the feeling of the body releasing sand through its pores. Visualize a calm, peaceful place, and include all of the sights, sounds and sensations of this image. Continue the deep breathing, and take a few minutes to continue this with closed eyes. When all is well again, return to the test.

If a "blanking" occurs for a certain question, skip it and move on to the next question. There will be time to return to the other question later. Get everything done that can be done, first, to guarantee all the grades that can be compiled, and to build all of the confidence possible. Then return to the weaker questions to build the marks from there.

Remember, one's own reality can be created, so as long as the belief is there, success will follow. And remember: anxiety can happen later, right now, there's an exam to be written!

After the examination is complete, whether there is a feeling for a good grade or a bad grade, don't dwell on the exam, and be certain to follow through on the reward that was promised…and enjoy it! Don't dwell on any mistakes that have been made, as there is nothing that can be done at this point anyway.

Additionally, don't begin to study for the next test right away. Do something relaxing for a while, and let the mind relax and prepare itself to begin absorbing information again.

From the results of the exam - both the grade and the entire experience, be certain to learn from what has gone on. Perfect studying habits and work some more on confidence in order to make the next examination experience even better than the last one.

Learn to avoid places where openings occurred for laziness, procrastination and day dreaming.

Use the time between this exam and the next one to better learn to relax, even learning to relax on cue, so that any anxiety can be controlled during the next exam. Learn how to relax the body. Slouch in your chair if that helps. Tighten and then relax all of the different muscle groups, one group at a time, beginning with the feet and then working all the way up to the neck and face. This will ultimately relax the muscles more than they were to begin with. Learn how to breathe deeply and comfortably, and focus on this breathing going in and out as a relaxing thought. With every exhale, repeat the word "relax."

As common as test anxiety is, it is very possible to overcome it. Make yourself one of the test-takers who overcome this frustrating hindrance.

Special Report: Federal Regulations - Staying Alert and Fit to Drive

Driving a commercial vehicle requires skill, education and physical fitness. Driving for long hours is tiring and even the best drivers will become less alert. You can cope with fatigue and maximize your alertness by following the federal regulations on hours of service and off duty time. You can also combat fatigue and maximize your alertness by maintaining a healthy lifestyle.

Federal Regulations on Hours of Service and Off-Duty Time

In an effort to control driver fatigue, the federal government established regulations governing hours of service and required off-duty time. These regulations specify driving time, off-duty time and prohibit driving after you have been on-duty in excess of specified amounts of time. Although these regulations once applied only to drivers who crossed state lines, in most states they now apply to all drivers, even those who operate solely within a single state.

- **On-duty time** refers to all the time, including driving time, that you perform work for a motor carrier. It also includes the time that you are required to stay with your assigned vehicle. And, it includes time that you perform paid work of any other kind--for example, a second job.
- **Driving time** refers to the total amount of time you spend at the controls of a commercial vehicle in operation.
- **7/8 consecutive days** refers to the period of time beginning at the day and time designated by the motor carrier as a period of 24 consecutive hours.

Under the Federal Regulations:
- You may not drive more than 11 hours following your last period of 8 consecutive hours off duty.
- You may not drive after being on duty (driving plus all other work) for 15 hours following your last 8 consecutive hours off-duty.
- You may not drive after being on-duty for 60 hours in any period of 7 consecutive days. However, if the company operates vehicles every day of the week, you may not drive after being on duty 70 hours in a period of 8 consecutive days. Before driving again, you must have sufficient time off to be in compliance with the hours of service limits.

Staying Alert:
- **Get enough rest.** When you go off duty, your first concern should be to get enough rest so that you will have the 7 to 8 hours sleep that every person needs. After you have gotten your sleep and you have been awake and alert for more than 8 hours without being notified of your next assignment, take a short nap so you will be alert when you return to work. Remember, sleep is the only way to overcome fatigue.
- **Schedule your trips safely.** Ideally, you should try to schedule trips for the hours when you are normally awake. However, many motor carriers operate around the clock. Therefore, you must be prepared to drive safely during irregular work times.
- **Rest during your off-duty times.** Everyone is affected by the circadian rhythm. This is the name of the 24-hour cycle of alertness that affects everyone. Normally, most people have low points of alertness from 2 to 6 a.m. and from 2 to 5 p.m. If you are already tired, your risk of falling asleep during these periods is greatly increased. That's why it's so important

to get as much rest as possible during your off-duty hours. Remember, many heavy vehicle crashes occur between midnight and 6 a.m.

- **Take a nap.** If you get sleepy, a short nap will do more for you than a cup of coffee. Find a safe place to pull over and stop. Remember, parking on the shoulder of an interstate or other main highway is dangerous and is not permitted except in an emergency. Napping is not considered an emergency. Find a rest area, truck stop or a safe place along a nearby road.
- **Avoid drugs.** No drugs can help you overcome being tired. Stimulants may keep you awake for a while; but, they won't make you alert. When they wear off, you'll be even more tired than if you had never taken them. Sleep is the only thing that will overcome fatigue.
- **Avoid medication.** Many medications can make you sleepy. These medications usually have a label or folder that warns against operating vehicles or machinery while taking them. Cold pills are one of the most common medicines that will make you sleepy. If you must drive with a cold, you are better off suffering from the cold than from the effects of the medicine.
- **Keep cool.** A hot, poorly ventilated cab can make you sleepy. Keep the window or vent cracked, or use the air conditioner.
- **Take a break.** Stay alert by stopping for a short break every 2 to 3 hours. Walk around and give your vehicle a safety check.

Drinking and Driving

From 1991 to 2012, over 12,500 people were killed each year because of drivers who had been drinking. About one-third of all fatal crashes involve drinking drivers. Be sure that you know the facts.

The Truth about Alcohol

FALSE	TRUE
A few drinks will improve your driving.	Alcohol is a drug that will make you less alert and reduce your ability to drive safely.
Some people can drink a lot and not feel the effects.	Everyone who drinks alcohol is affected. Just one drink affects your ability to drive safely.
If you eat a lot, you won't get as drunk.	Food will not keep you from getting drunk.
Coffee and fresh air will help you get sober.	Only time will help you get sober. Other methods don't work.
Stick with beer. It's not as strong as wine or whiskey.	A 12 -ounce glass of beer, a five-ounce glass of wine and a shot of liquor have the same amount of alcohol.

Just one alcoholic drink can affect your driving ability. Even a small amount of alcohol affects the brain. Alcohol first affects the part of the brain that controls judgment and self-control. This can keep you from knowing when you are getting drunk. Alcohol affects your judgment and driving ability. Your chances of being in a crash are eight times greater if you drive after drinking than if you drive sober.

Alcohol also affects coordination, reaction time and vision. Ninety percent of the information used in driving comes from seeing. Alcohol relaxes the eye muscles. As a result, you cannot focus properly. Any restriction in vision could cause you to crash.

Blood alcohol content (BAC) is the amount of alcohol in your body. BAC depends on the amount of alcohol consumed, the time spent drinking and your body weight. The more you drink, the higher your BAC will be and the more affected your driving will become.

It takes about one hour for the blood stream to rid itself of one once of alcohol. For example, if you drink three beers, it will take approximately three hours for your body to rid itself of the alcohol. Only time can get rid of the effects of alcohol. Coffee, cold showers or exercise will not make you sober.

Mixing alcohol with other drugs usually multiplies the effects of both. Having one drink and taking an aspirin or simple cold pill could have the same effect as several drinks.

Almost any drug can reduce your ability to drive safely. It's not just illegal drugs that cause problems. Many over-the-counter drugs and prescription drugs can cause sleepiness and dizziness. These drugs often affect your alertness and reaction time.

Read the label before taking any drug or medicine. Look for warnings about the side effects. If you are uncertain about the effects of a drug, ask your doctor or pharmacist.

Laws prohibit possession and use of many drugs while you are on duty. It's illegal to be under the influence of any controlled substance, narcotic or other substance that can make a driver unsafe. This includes prescription and over-the-counter drugs that may make you sleepy or affect your driving ability. Possession and use of a drug is legal if your doctor tells you that the drug will not affect your driving ability.

Alcohol and drug testing. Federal regulations require that drivers be tested for misuse of alcohol and the use of controlled substances such as amphetamines, marijuana, opiates, PCP and cocaine.

- Testing for misuse of alcohol:
- on a random basis
- for reasonable suspicion of misuse
- following a crash, and
- when returning to duty.
- You may be tested for controlled substances:
- prior to employment
- on a random basis
- for reasonable suspicion of use
- following a crash, and
- when returning to duty

Promptly follow your employer's instructions for alcohol and drug testing. Violation of the regulations for alcohol and drug use and testing can jeopardize your career as a commercial driver.

Special Report: Potential New Highway Safety Rules Get Tough on Commercial Drivers

Offenses such as drunken driving, leaving the scene of an accident and excessive speeding — even if committed during off-duty hours — could cost a commercial truck driver his job. A proposed U.S. Federal Motor Carrier Safety Administration (FMCSA), Washington, D.C., rule would require states to suspend or revoke a driver's commercial license for traffic violations committed in any vehicle.

Currently, the Commercial Motor Vehicle Safety Act of 1986 (CMVSA) lists eight offenses for which a commercial driver could be disqualified, including reckless driving, mistakes leading to fatal accidents and using a commercial vehicle to commit a felony. The new rule, which complies with the U.S. Congress' Motor Carrier Safety Improvement Act of 1999, applies the 1986 CMVSA standards to violations committed in any vehicle.

"The FMCSA believes that a record of convictions for serious traffic violations and other offenses while operating a non-commercial motor vehicle is just as important as a conviction in a commercial motor vehicle in determining whether a driver should retain his or her [commercial driver's license (CDL)]," the proposed rule states.

While trucking industry associations and drivers' representatives do not oppose the new rule, some believe that it is "feel-good legislation."

"From our perspective, it's a lot of regulatory overkill," says Todd Spencer, executive vice president of the Owner-Operators and Independent Drivers Association (OOIDA), Grain Valley, Mo. "I am unaware of any state that does not already suspend or disqualify commercial drivers for these convictions. It wouldn't make any difference what they drove."

But the FMCSA's David Longo says the issue is more complicated. "What happens in real life is that the driver will say to the judge, 'you will be taking away my livelihood if you revoke my CDL.'" Then the judge may decide to substitute a driving course or a probation period for a suspension, thus masking the violation on the driver's record.

The new rule, Longo says, would eliminate such loopholes. "This is going to require states to do something," he adds. Under the proposed rule, "the conviction must show up on a driver's commercial license, and the states are compelled to create a mechanism within their databases to allow for the transfer."

Despite such mandates, the new rule presents logistical problems, according to Elisa Braver, senior epidemiologist for the Insurance Institute for Highway Safety, Arlington, Va. "You have to be very aware of the limitations of driver records," she says. "For example, if someone is convicted of a violation in a state other than the state in which he or she is licensed, then there could be problems. It's a constant struggle to have accurate driver records."

Different states do not necessarily code violations in the same ways, says OOIDA's Spencer. "A parking ticket in one state can be a moving violation in another. It's frustrating, particularly for truckers," who constantly are crossing state lines.

Additionally, long-haul truck drivers do not receive equal protection under the current traffic court system, Spencer says. "A truck driver might be 1,500 miles away on his or her court date. The people who write the tickets know that out-of-town drivers most likely will not make the court date."

By raising the stakes of traffic violations, however, the new rule could encourage truck drivers to forego business trips to be in court. "When the penalties get so significant, you have to be there," Spencer says.

Nevertheless, Spencer says he wonders whether safety rules targeting only commercial truck drivers are missing part of the picture. "The vast majority of accidents where trucks are involved actually are caused by someone driving an automobile," he says.

The statistics on large-truck crashes prove that commercial truck drivers should be required to drive more safely than most drivers, Braver says. "In two-vehicle crashes involving a large truck and a passenger vehicle, 98 percent of deaths occur to passenger vehicle occupants," she says.

Braver says she is not aware of studies that compare a driver's off-duty driving performance to commercial driving performance, but she notes that drivers with a history of traffic citations are at a higher risk for future citations and crashes. But "the majority of crashes involve drivers who have had no citations or police-reported crashes in the previous three years," she adds.

Statisticians at the FMCSA predict that the new rule, if approved, would prevent at least 500 truck-related accidents per year.

Special Report: Overview of US Trucking Industry

Size Statistics

In the U.S., the trucking industry as a whole has employed an estimated 9 million Americans. Out of the 9 million, UPS employs 60,000 of them. There are close to 15.5 million trucks operated in the United States alone, including 2 million tractors. Nation-wide, there are close to 3.5 million truck drivers who operate in the industry. Of the 3.5 million, almost 400,000 are independent truck drivers. There are over 1.2 million trucking companies in the U.S. Although, 96% of the 1.2 million operate fewer than 30 trucks, and 82% operate fewer than 10.

Financial Statistics

Total revenue estimates for the trucking industry are 255.5 billion. For Hire or Common Carriers Trucking companies generated revenue estimated at 97.9 billion. Private Fleets generated revenue estimated at 121 billion. Truck drivers make, on average, 30.3 cents each mile. Their yearly average is 32,000 dollars a year. To operate on U.S. roads, truck industries pay about 21 billion dollars.

Accident Statistics

The United States has more than 200,000,000 licensed drivers. There are close to 7 million vehicle accidents a year, and around 44,000 vehicle-related deaths a year. Not even 10% of these deaths involve commercial vehicles. Almost 5,000 people are killed in truck accidents every year. 98% of the time, the one who dies is the one driving the other vehicle.

Fuel Statistics

12.8% of all fuel purchased in the United States is bought by the trucking industry. Automobiles and light vehicles accounted for 63% of the fuel purchased.

Sales Statistics

In the U.S., there are almost 200,000 trucks and 280,000 trailers sold each year.

Emergency Road Call Statistics

<u>What percentage of problems occur on the road?</u>
- Tires - 51.3%
- Jump or Pull start - 7.6%
- Air Line or hose - 4.7%
- Alternator - 4.1%
- Wiring - 3.9%
- Fuel Filter R/R - 3.7%
- Fuel - 3.5%
- Brake - 2.4%
- All Others are less than 1%

Special Report: Suspension of a Commercial Driver's License (CDL)

A commercial driver has a period of ten days to request a driver's license hearing after receiving a DC-28 form that is entitled Officer's Certification. The request for driver's license hearing for a commercial driver's license must follow the same format as described for a regular driver's license. The administrative hearing for the commercial driver's license may consider different facts and requires different proof than for a non-commercial driver's license. A timely, written request for hearing must be provided for both the normal non-commercial driver's license and the commercial driver's license.

A commercial driver's licensee may not drive, operate, or be in physical control of a commercial vehicle while having any alcohol in the driver's system. A commercial driver will be placed out of service for twenty-four hours if there is any alcohol in the driver's system unless an alcohol test shows a reading of 0.04 or greater or unless there is an alcohol test refusal. If the out of service order is violated, a first conviction results in a ninety day commercial driving disqualification, with a second conviction resulting in a year disqualification and the third resulting in a three year disqualification.

No person may drive a commercial motor vehicle with an alcohol concentration of 0.04 or more while driving or as measured within two hours of driving or if the driver violated the standard DUI statute or ordinance. A first violation is a misdemeanor with a sentence of not less than forty-eight consecutive hours in jail or less than six months and a fine of not less than $200 or more than $500 in addition to penalties that would apply to the DUI law for non-commercial drivers.

A commercial driver will be disqualified from driving a commercial vehicle for not less than one year on the first occurrence and for life (which may be reduced to not less than ten years under certain circumstances) after a second offense if the person is convicted of having an alcohol concentration of 0.04 or more at the time of driving a commercial motor vehicle, is convicted of having an alcohol concentration of 0.04 or more as measured within two hours of driving a commercial vehicle, is convicted of DUI while driving a commercial motor vehicle, is convicted of leaving the scene of an accident involving a commercial motor vehicle, is convicted of using a commercial motor vehicle in the commission of any felony or the person refuses a blood or breath test.

A commercial driver's license implied consent advisory must be read to the commercial driver before administering the alcohol test. This implied consent advisory is separate from the normal implied consent advisory to a non-commercial driver. Both implied consent advisories must be given to the commercial driver in written form and read to the commercial driver.

If a commercial driver's license is suspended, a driver may still be eligible to drive a non-commercial vehicle under current interpretation of the law. For this reason, a timely written request for administrative hearing should be requested in accordance with the procedures for requesting a hearing. Time is of the essence. You may lose your right to drive for your living if you do not act quickly and properly.

Special Report: Is the Commercial Driver's License Program Flawed?

In New Mexico, an eighteen year old with 17 previous driver's license suspensions drove a tractor-trailer that was involved in a fatal crash. In Illinois, a trucker who collided with an Amtrak train in a crash that killed 11 persons was driving with a special permit that he had obtained even though his commercial driver's license had been suspended. And in more than a dozen states, hundreds of unqualified drivers were able to fraudulently obtain licenses for commercial vehicles, leading to at least nine highway deaths.

Almost a decade after the commercial driver's license program was put into place to make the nation's highways safer, the system is so flawed that it is allowing dangerous truckers to remain on the road. Although the program has successfully rooted out truckers who held multiple licenses in more than one state, oversight is so lax that scams to obtain bogus licenses are commonplace.

A recent Pennsylvania scheme showed the commercial driver's license system could be vulnerable to terrorists intent on turning 18-wheelers into weapons of mass destruction. In addition, commercial licenses are so easy to keep that truckers with terrible driving records and even drunken driving convictions are able to stay on the road. Under the commercial driver's license program, each state is supposed to keep a database of truckers licensed in that state, record all convictions those truckers receive in that state, and share the information with other states. That way, states can identify bad drivers and get them off the road.

But states don't always know about their own bad drivers, according to an audit released last year by the Department of Transportation's Office of Inspector General. That happens because states in which violations occur are sometimes way behind in recording them or just don't bother doing it, the inspector general found.

"We have the appearance of a safe system," said Dieter Harper of the Inspector General's Chicago office. "But when you start digging, you find out that you've got untrained operators, you've got minimum-wage employees, you've got no employees to do that kind of entry."

In other cases, states knew about convictions as serious as driving under the influence of drugs -- but didn't do anything about them. The inspector general also found that more than two dozen states "masked" traffic convictions by withholding them from truckers' driving records.

Masking works this way: A trucker is cited for reckless driving, but instead of reporting the violation, the state or county dismisses the citation if the trucker attends driving school or commits no more violations in that jurisdiction within a specified period. That means a trucker could be cited for speeding in five counties and reckless driving in three others, all in a few months, and none of the violations would appear on his record.

"The drivers, with the aid of the courts, are hiding numerous serious traffic violations," said Teri Graham, director of the Federal Motor Carrier Safety Administration's Kansas office. "That's a very big problem, because it allows some real bad drivers to stay on the road."

Special treatment

Many states also allow drivers to avoid disqualification through special licenses or permits to operate commercial vehicles, according to the inspector general. A trucker who was struck by an Amtrak train in a crash that killed 11 persons in March 1999 in Bourbonnais, Ill., was operating under a probationary license -- even though his commercial driver's license had been suspended for multiple moving violations, the inspector general said.

"Such cases aren't unusual," said Harper, whose office investigated the crash.

In some cases, even when numerous tickets and suspensions made it onto their records, truckers still had valid commercial driver's licenses, according to an examination of accident reports by The Kansas City Star. One driver whose license had been suspended 17 times was in an accident in Albuquerque, N.M., on Jan. 16, 1999, that killed a 16-year-old girl. The truck driver, who was only 18, had been involved in two previous accidents, records show.

New Mexico authorities said the trucker had a valid license at the time of the crash. The suspensions, they said, were for the driver's failure to appear in court for citations issued from 1996 through 1998. The state Transportation Department couldn't explain how he was able to obtain a commercial driver's license with such a poor record.

And in March 1999, a trucker in a 1999 Peterbilt turned left on U.S. 95 in Nevada in front of a sport-utility vehicle. The SUV crashed into the truck, killing the 65-year-old driver and her 69-year-old husband. The trucker, 40, had 10 previous license suspensions and had been involved in two prior accidents, records show.

An official in the truck safety agency's Nevada office said the commercial driver's license program had so many holes that he wasn't surprised the driver was able to keep his license. The inspector general's audit blamed state programs and lax federal oversight for allowing thousands of dangerous truckers to remain on the highways.

In July, the truck safety agency -- at the order of Congress -- proposed rules to help close some of the loopholes in the commercial driver's license system. States would be prohibited from withholding convictions from a driver's record, and truckers would face tougher penalties for driving after their commercial driver's license has been revoked or suspended.

The agency is reviewing public comments before issuing a final rule. The agency estimates that the measures would result in the revocation of nearly 32,000 commercial driver's licenses a year.

License Scams

The commercial driver's license program also is mired in licensing scandals. In 1998, investigators found that employees in the Illinois secretary of state's office were taking cash bribes in exchange for passing grades on commercial driver's license tests.

The investigation expanded when authorities discovered that examiners in Florida had helped applicants from more than 25 states establish false residency in Florida, get their Florida commercial driver's licenses and then exchange them for licenses in their home states. The scandal has resulted in the indictments or convictions of more than 40 persons.

In a Georgia plot, an examiner sold more than 500 licenses, and in August, an examiner in Ohio pleaded guilty to falsifying 248 commercial licenses. The truck safety agency says at least nine highway deaths can be traced to drivers who illegally obtained commercial driver's licenses through such scams.

Six of those deaths occurred on Nov. 8, 1994.

Ricardo Guzman was driving a tractor-trailer along Interstate 94 south of Milwaukee when, according to police records, other truckers began honking and warning him over their CBs that a steel taillight/mud flap assembly was falling off his rig. Guzman, who spoke little English and later said his CB was broken, kept driving.

The hunk of metal fell off and was hit by a Plymouth minivan carrying the Rev. Duane and Janet Willis and their six children, ages 6 weeks to 13 years.

The 60-pound metal piece ricocheted under the van, puncturing the gas tank and turning the vehicle into a fireball. A witness caught Janet Willis as she ran from the van with her clothes on fire and helped her roll on the ground to put out the flames. The parents escaped with severe burns, but five of their children burned to death in the van -- the baby still strapped in his car seat. The sixth child died the next day.

Investigators said Guzman had obtained his commercial driver's license from an examiner who had helped more than 80 applicants get passing grades on written and driving tests. Although the examiner said in a sworn statement that Guzman had been among the 80, Guzman's lawyer said that had never been proved and that Guzman had passed the necessary tests legitimately. According to a federal crash database analyzed by The Star, Guzman had been involved in four previous accidents in the two years leading up to the accident.

The commercial driver's license scheme in Pennsylvania came to light after the recent terrorist attacks.

According to court documents, 20 men worked through a middleman to illegally obtain commercial driver's licenses, 18 with hazardous materials endorsements. Authorities feared the suspects could have been part of a scheme to use trucks in another wave of attacks, but later said that the men weren't part of any terrorist plot.

Prompted by the inspector general and a federal panel, the truck safety agency says it will crack down on states that fail to correct problems.

Special Report: New Commercial Driver's License Regulations

The Federal Motor Carrier Safety Administration (FMCSA) recently promulgated new commercial driver's license regulations that became effective on September 30, 2002.

The FMCSA issued the new regulations in accordance with the requirements of Motor Carrier Safety Improvement Act (MCSIA) of 1999, which directed the FMCSA to make significant revisions to the CDL program. These regulations provide, among other things, for the suspension or permanent revocation of commercial driver's licenses for convictions of serious traffic violations committed while operating non-commercial vehicles.

The new regulations expand the definition of serious traffic violation. Serious traffic violation means conviction of any of the following offenses:
- Excessive speeding, involving any single offense for any speed of 15 miles per hour or more above the posted speed limit
- Reckless driving
- Improper or erratic traffic lane changes
- Following the vehicle ahead too closely
- A violation, arising in connection with a fatal accident, of State or local law relating to motor vehicle traffic control
- Driving a CMV without obtaining a CDL
- Driving a CMV without a CDL in the driver's possession. Any individual who provides proof to the enforcement authority that issued the citation, by the date the individual must appear in court or pay any fine for such a violation, that the individual held a valid CDL on the date the citation was issued, shall not be guilty of this offense
- Driving a CMV without the proper class of CDL and/or endorsements for the specific vehicle group being operated or for the passengers or type of cargo being transported

The Final Rule imposes mandatory periods of disqualification that are identical regardless of whether the serious traffic violations were committed while the driver is operating a CMV or a non-CMV. In the case of a conviction for driving under the influence or refusing to be tested, the Final Rule imposes a one-year mandatory disqualification period for the first offense (a "major" offense), and imposes a lifetime disqualification for a second offense. The Final Rule also establishes mandatory periods of disqualification based on two or more convictions of serious traffic violations committed within a three-year period.

Disqualification for such convictions apply regardless of whether the individual's license was revoked, cancelled, or suspended. For disqualification purposes, convictions for out-of-state violations are treated the same as convictions for violations that are committed in the home State.

Each State has the authority to set additional disqualification requirements for drivers licensed in the State. The Final Rule sets the minimum disqualification requirements for a State to remain in compliance. States that do not comply with the Final Rule within three years may have Motor Carrier Safety Assistance Program grant funds withheld.

The new regulations also establish FMCSA authority for imposing an emergency disqualification of CDL drivers imposing an "imminent hazard". Imminent hazard means the existence of a condition that presents a substantial likelihood that death, serious illness, severe personal injury, or a substantial endangerment to health, property, or the environment may occur before the reasonably foreseeable completion date of a formal proceeding begun to lessen the risk that death, illness, injury or endangerment. The period of emergency disqualification cannot exceed 30 days unless the FMCSA provides the driver with notice of the disqualification and a hearing to present a defense to the proposed disqualification.

Finally, other changes brought about by the new regulations include: 1) States are prohibited from issuing a special CDL or permit (including a provisional or temporary license) to any CDL driver who is disqualified or who has his or her non-CDL or driving privilege revoked, suspended, or canceled; 2) States are prohibited from "masking" convictions required to be maintained or transmitted to the State where the driver is licensed and from using diversion programs or any other disposition that would defer the listing of a guilty verdict on a CDL driver's record; and 3) applicants for an initial CDL, and those transferring or renewing a CDL, must provide the State with the name of all States where previously licensed to drive for the past ten years any type of motor vehicle, allowing State officials to obtain an applicant's complete driving record.

On behalf of its affiliated unions (including the IUOE), the Transportation Trades Department of the AFL-CIO has filed a Petition for Reconsideration of the Final Rule with the FMCSA.

Additional Bonus Material

Due to our efforts to try to keep this book to a manageable length, we've created a link that will give you access to all of your additional bonus material.

Please visit http://www.mometrix.com/bonus948/cdlspt to access the information.

CPSIA information can be obtained
at www.ICGtesting.com
Printed in the USA
LVHW10*1823150818
587064LV00017B/238/P

9 781516 707942